Software Engineering

for Students

by Michael Coleman
and Stephen Pratt

School of Information Science,
Portsmouth Polytechnic

Chartwell-Bratt   Studentlitteratur

©Chartwell-Bratt (Publishing & Training) Limited
ISBN 0-86238-115-0

Studentlitteratur
ISBN 91-44-26031-8

Printed in Sweden by Studentlitteratur
Lund 1986

DEDICATION

To -

Jennifer, Stephen and Catherine C. ... and Fred(a)

         and

Jo and Jake P. ... and ?

Contents

Preface

SECTION III: SOFTWARE IMPLEMENTATION ISSUES

Preface

Since the term was coined in 1968, software engineering has been described variously as an 'emergent', 'emerging' and 'new' discipline. The adjective is of little concern; the important, and appropriate, word is discipline. The successful production of complex, and not-so-complex, software is only possible through the application of a disciplined approach to the job; and since the needs of industry for well-qualified software engineers continue to mount, the subject is worthy of regard as an academic discipline.

This book aims to cover both aspects of software engineering. Intended as an introductory text for all students taking a course in this subject, it covers both the principles and the practices of software engineering. The treatment, whilst covering such important areas as project management and quality assurance, focusses primarily on the topics to which students will most easily relate: programming and documentation. In this respect only a general knowledge of (BBC) BASIC and/or Pascal is needed as a necessary pre-requisite.

Apart from each other, the authors would like to extend especial thanks to Tania Austwick, Dave Early, Ken LeFevre and John Moore - whose assistance in the preparation of this book extended way above the call of bribery.

Michael Coleman, Stephen Pratt

15th August 1986

CHAPTER ONE

The Need for Software Engineering

"Life is just one damned thing after another"

Frank Ward O'Malley

1.1 The Project Life-cycle Illustrated

To understand the necessity for an organised, disciplined and structured approach to software production, one must first experience the effects of producing complex software in an ad hoc fashion. Many of the problems encountered relate to the industrial environment in which such software is produced and, for this reason, are difficult for the student to appreciate at this stage. In this chapter, therefore, we will try to indicate the scale of the trouble caused by ad hoc methods of software production by means of a blow-by-blow account of a process with which the student is undoubtedly familiar: the production of a single, simple program as a coursework assignment.

Consider the following scenario: You are set a particular problem, the solution of which requires you to write and document a program. You own, or have access to, a microcomputer with the necessary software to enable you to write and run a program, interactively using keyboard and monitor, and produce hardcopy listings. Figure 1.1 (affectionately known as the Submit Loop) summarises the sequence of events normally encountered from the time the problem was received to its submission for assessment. A description of the typical experiences during each of the identified phases is given.

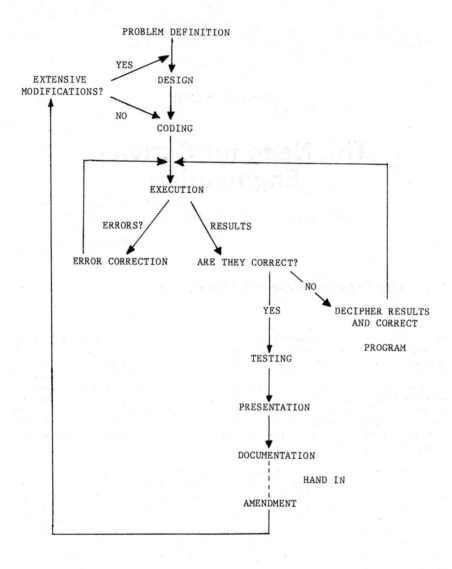

Fig 1.1   Submit Loop

2

1.1.1 PROBLEM DEFINITION

In some shape or form, a description of the problem to be solved will have been suplied. It may have been an exercise taken out of a book or one which has been invented. It is most likely to have been described purely in functional terms; that is, with no constraints set on such things as: how fast the program has to be, or how short it has to be, what restrictions there are to be placed on the ranges of input data values, what documentation standards are expected, what presentation format is required, or on what programming approach should be adopted. In short, one or two unanswered questions may remain.

1.1.2 DESIGN

A perhaps undeservedly superior term used to describe the drafting of an initial solution on paper. In its original form it is usually an illegible diagram which attempts to highlight the individual functions to be performed, along with their interconnections. Traditionally the diagram is in the form of a flowchart, although you wouldn't know that by looking at it since the symbols invariably do not conform to any notational standard. Often the diagram almost assumes the proportions of a work of surrealist art, fully understood only by its creator. From this design is to emerge a fully coded program.

1.1.3 CODING

This is an empirical phase in which the flowchart gets translated into a program, usually on odd pieces of paper which are liberally distributed about the work area. During this stage some of the aspects identified in the flowchart get lost in translation, i.e. design refinements are continually introduced. Some components which were not present in the original design get incorporated. The rationale for the inclusion of many program statements will not exist on paper, making design ratification very difficult.

The overriding aim is to get the program into a state in which it can be submitted to the computer, as soon as possible. ('State' being the operative word.) As a consequence no attention is given to the way it is written, or how a solution has been approached. The inclusion of any comments during this or any of the subsequent refinement stages, except the final presentation stage, is likely to be by accident.

The choice over what programming language statements should be used will be determined by the confidence accumulated to date with certain instructions. Because of the need to get the program working as soon as possible this will not be seen as the time to adopt a heuristic approach.

For those lacking any formal training in computer programming there will be a subconscious tendency to use statements that have a day-to-day decision-making ring of familiarity: IF 'something' THEN 'do something else', GOTO 'some destination', etc. At the end of this stage something will have been written down which can be submitted to the computer.

Of course, some will miss out the paper part of this stage altogether, preferring to key their program code into the computer as it is devised. In such cases no documentary evidence will exist, even on the floor.

1.1.4 EXECUTION

This is the stage which is often regarded as the most productive, simply because you are doing something physical at a terminal. The act of typing at the machine is often felt to be a most fruitful activity: I am keying, therefore I am computing. Unfortunately the opposite could well be the case. Submitting the program to the computer is often the most unproductive stage, since through sheer enthusiasm (not to mention the opportunity for on-line redesign (undocumented)) all sorts of errors can introduced. The psychological pressure is on; it is imperative that the program is typed in as quickly as possible and the results of the first run obtained - let's put it in and see what happens.

1.1.5 ERROR CORRECTION

The initial outcome of the execution phase will be somewhere between a handful and an armful of errors. After coming to terms with the inconceivable - that after spending so much time (not to mention love and care) on designing a solution, writing the program and typing it in, that it simply doesn't work - you realise that it is time to sit down with a manual and try to decipher the error messages and investigate the causes.

Many of them are found to be due to simple typing errors (like 0 for O and I for 1), others are simply attributable to the fact that the instructions do not exist. During the first pass of the Submit Loop most of the errors are simple to find, in any case the tendency is to correct half of them and hope the rest will go away. Funnily enough, sometimes they do. So it's GOTO the EXECUTION Phase and try your luck again.

Not surprisingly, perhaps, the more times this stage is experienced, the easier it becomes to diagnose and correct the error messages. Time in this stage gets shorter and shorter: I'm becoming a real programmer! Real programmers don't meet this stage at all.

1.1.6 INITIAL VALIDATION

The euphoric stage - the program is running and some results have been obtained. Unfortunately the euphoria is short-lived. The results are not what were expected - either because they don't match the answers in the book or those that somebody else has got. So what is wrong? Is it the program, the input data, the answer(s) you are comparing yours with - or are they all wrong?

It's validating-the-program time. Firstly you have to establish a set of results that are known to be correct. Armed with these the program is then checked by performing a dry run with the data values originally submitted to it. If the program is small then this task is relatively simple. On the other hand if it is a complex program then more output may be required than has been printed so far. So you either turn to a trace/debugging facility that is available on your computer, or incorporate your own by saturating your program with print/write statements (i.e. introducing the diagnostic statements missing from the original design).

In either case you eventually pin it down to a mistake in your program outline, or the value/format of the input data, or in the transcription to the programming language, or in the expected answer. In the latter case you would eventually GOTO the TESTING Stage. In all other cases you will correct the mistake(s) and GOTO the EXECUTION Stage - again.

A keyboard fanatic would have tried a few instant solutions in the form of alternative instructions or data values, and hoped for the best. If (and when) these failed to do the trick, the next step would be to look for Somebody With An Answer, since the taking of a logical and disciplined approach to the problem would not be an item on the agenda.

1.1.7 TESTING

This stage is not usually experienced by the unenthusiastic, since it is here that the inherent strengths and weaknesses of the program are fully determined. Alternative input data sets are accumulated and submitted to the program which is then executed the requisite number of times. The results are gathered and compared with the expected test answers and from these a figure of merit determined for the program.

Typical tests on the program would, for instance, include those to see if there were any checks performed on the boundaries of the input data values, as well as tests to determine whether the algorithms were sufficiently robust to cope with the data values on the extremes of their boundaries. These test values would have been obtained from experts, text books, or for those sufficiently knowledgable in the field, have been self-generated. Irrespective of their origin, considerable confidence over the values, and expected results, is required to validate a program. The detection of any deficiency in the progam would result in remedial action.

The only thing that drives you on during this phase is the desire to do a thorough, professional job. Knowing that it is the best you can do is what provides the job satisfaction - praise or thanks comes (if it does) as a bonus. After thorough testing, then, GOTO the PRESENTATION Stage.

1.1.8 PRESENTATION

By now the program is assumed to be working satisfactorily. For the typical student assignment, it is at this point that comments are added, layout adjusted to make it more readable (e.g. indentation) and the variable names are changed so as to be a bit more meaningful (and less obscene). The input and output formats are made prettier, meaningful and a lot more presentable. The diagnostic statements are discarded. The enthusiasts do as much as they can simply to do as good a job as possible; the others do as much as is thought necessary to convince the assessor that this is the product of many diligent hours. The enthusiasts often adopt such a presentable approach in all phases, paying dividends by maximising visibilty.

1.1.9 DOCUMENTATION

After the program has been through all this it is time to 'do the documentation.' This amounts to redrawing (or drawing for the first time) the flowcharts, and the writing of a descriptive piece about each section of the program.

It is now that you realise that the final program bears no resemblance whatsoever to the original design. All the alterations have been done in code, there is no record of the history of development or the rationale behind the insertion/deletion of certain instructions. This isn't surprising since there aren't many people who want to document their mistakes. But are they mistakes or just intermediate phases of program development? Certainly some of the stages of the Submit Loop, particularly validation, would have caused less pain if there had been documentation to use.

The documentation of a program is usually left until last because it is considered a boring job with no apparent rewards, especially when it is done for what has now become a big program. The consolation is that it is the end, it is the last you are going to see of it, no more tinkering and no more edits.

Oops. Unfortunately you haven't finished with this program after all. In his infinite wisdom your mentor has set another exercise which involves an extension to cater for options that weren't in the original problem definition, e.g. instead of running the program for ten numbers run it for twenty. (There could be lots of other reasons which are self-generated. It might occur to you, some months later, that the program could be used in another application area if only it were given a few extra facilities; or even that it forms the starting point for a suite of programs to comprise a major undergraduate project.)

In the first case, there is a definite psychological element associated with being asked to alter/amend a program believed to be complete. Having to go back over ground can easily influence the quality of work done since it is invariably a task undertaken with reluctance. Nevertheless the job has to be done, and done thoroughly: altering array and variable declarations, ensuring that any violation of the input data checks is remedied, altering the output phase to accommodate newly generated data values, ensuring that the algorithms can cope with the new demands and that the control flow through the program is correct.

At some time during this stage a sobering thought will make its entrance - that any amendment made to the program has repercussioms at all stages of the Submit Loop (and that includes documentation!) The effect at each stage depends heavily upon how far-reaching the amendments are, e.g. can the program be modified easily, or does it have to be redesigned from scratch. Whatever the case, it is imperative that a note be made of all changes just in case the problem gets redefined yet again at a later date. So it is either GOTO DESIGN or, GOTO CODING. Isn't it demoralising?

1.2 Small Projects and Large Projects

So far we have illustrated in some detail the experiences gained from producing a single, simple program. Experiences gained with more complex systems are very similar to those discussed above, except that there are a lot more of them. The intention now is to build upon what has been said previously by highlighting some of the idiosyncracies of large programming projects.

Basically, the development of a large program can be done in one of two ways. It can either be carried out completely by a single programmer, or broken down into a series of small programs which can be written by a number of programmers. However, the single programmer approach just isn't practical, since the time taken to produce such a large program could result in it being out of date before it was completed. The approach adopted has to be cost-effective in a market which is evolving as fast as computing. Splitting the program up means that the development of the individual programs can proceed in parallel, each with their own little life-cycle (or Submit Loop as it was called earlier), with the consequent saving in overall development time.

The simultaneous development of these programs is fine until it comes to the time when they have to be linked together to form a cohesive large program. It is at this stage that programs which have to work amicably together are discovered to be totally incompatible, either because of poor design or because the individual programmers have failed to communicate with each other. The thorough testing of one program is hard enough; the integration and testing of a number of programs can be a nightmare. So what is so different? In developing a single program the programmer sees the complete picture, whereas the programmer who is writing code for a component module of the big program only sees a small part of the big picture. To some extent the individual programmer works in isolation.

Clearly the difficulties associated with the integration and testing of a large program in this way are related to the number of personnel involved and, to a lesser extent, the size of the geographical area over which these people are spread. Also with the large program being developed by a number of people there has to be someone who takes on the responsibility of ensuring that they are all working towards the same ends.

Other factors influence the project development: the difficulties of programmers having to communicate with each other; overcoming the inevitable personality differences between people who have to work together; determining who fills the gap when somebody leaves and ensuring that it is possible to complete/correct their work. Clearly you cannot solely rely on verbal evidence of what has gone on before, particularly when it comes to the integration stage when all the little modules have to be linked together.

Good documentation is essential in this respect. Every member of the project team will depend on it for identifying modules and their function, hidden variable names, the interaction between modules, etc. Good documentation implies that it is understandable. To be understandable, by all concerned, means that it has to be produced to some form of standard, otherwise it could be worse than useless (mis-interpretation of the documentation could result in a program's condition actually deteriorating!) In a similar way the adoption of a common approach to the production of software is also advantageous.

1.3 The Software Crisis

As outlined above, the development of large programs as a series of small ones has many facets which need to be considered. When one considers an industrial environment, however, there are still further complications associated with the development of software.

Here the concern is not solely that of writing a complex program, but of developing a piece of software which is dependent upon the parallel development of the systems hardware. Consequently there are additional

8

problems for project management, such as the interfacing between hardware and software teams as well as within them. Unfortunately communication between teams is often left until the hardware and software components are integrated, at which time the detection of an error results in each side blaming the other. If the error can be corrected by changes in either software or hardware then the former usually loses, since it is generally easier and more cost-effective to make changes in software than in hardware. What tends to happen, therefore, is that the hardware team try and cast their design in 'stone' as soon as possible.

A variety of pressures are associated with the project as a whole. It will typically require the team to work to a tight deadline, must be cost-effective, incorporates the psychological aspects of personnel having their future tied to the success of the project, and so on. The involvement and affect of any one project member is no longer solely at a local level. The ramifications of any badly performed task can be felt throughout the whole project.

Figure 1.2 illustrates the various phases of the life-cycle of a typical industrial project, each of which we now consider in more detail.

1.3.1 FORMAL REQUEST

Before any detailed work can commence on a given project there must be a clear and concise statement of its scope and objectives. After all, in commerce it is more likely that a software project is going to be considered as a formal undertaking, rather than informal, purely on investment grounds. It is also likely that it is going to be considered on the grounds of future investment potential. All of which reinforce the case for a well-defined definition. Typically the written specification would contain the following information:

* Name and originator of the project.

* Project name and brief description.

* Intended scope - naming participating departments, development procedures to be adopted and timescales.

* Objectives of the system together with the reasons for initiating the project.

* Definition of the resource requirements, priority of the project in comparison to others, and funding for the initial study.

1.3.2 PRELIMINARY STUDY

At this stage a small team, or even a single person, would be assigned to

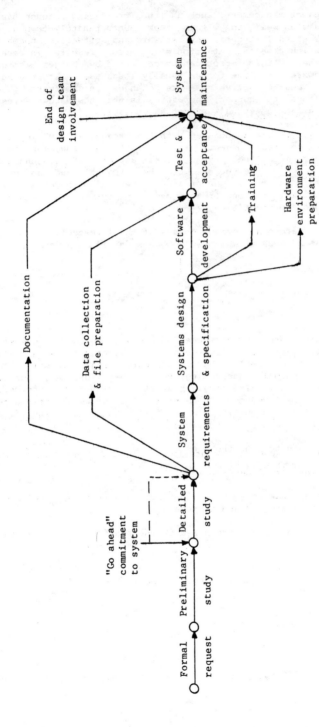

Fig 1.2   Project Life-Cycle: Schedule

perform an initial study the purpose of which would be to assess the feasibility of the project. This exercise would need to be performed as quickly as possible, and at low cost. The objectives of this stage would be to:

* Define the problem in technical terms, trying to highlight any unseen pitfalls.

* Assess possible further directions of investigation.

* Assess the feasiblity of a solution.

* Recommend to management a course of action - e.g. do nothing, modify existing procedures or investigate further.

1.3.3 DETAILED STUDY

The purpose of this stage is to uncover all the facts and opinions that may be used to define with the same clarity and precision what is required of the software system in terms of: function, performance, reliabilty and operating costs.

1.3.4 SYSTEM REQUIREMENTS

After analysing the results of the detailed study and having considerable discussion with the managerial and operational staff it is necessary to write a systems requirement document. Such a document should try to highlight the objectives set by management and any constraints set by management, highlight any constraints imposed by technical considerations, and list the requirements as shown by the detailed study to be essential. It is necessary that such a document should be agreed by all those involved - i.e. be seen as a form of contractual document.

1.3.5 SYSTEMS DESIGN AND SPECIFICATION

The design phase broadly consists of three sub-phases:

* Detailed consideration of the system requirements.

* The synthesis of a scheme to satisfy the requirements.

* The specification of the scheme.

Clearly this involves continued contact and discussion with both the management and operational staff of the user departments. Although the actual design process is difficult to formalise, it does have a tangible output in the form of a specification which does reflect the type of work undertaken during that stage. The exact form of the specification will vary considerably, however there will be a well-defined, rigidly enforced method of producing software (i.e. methodology) which is aimed at reducing the risk of errors of omission and commission. Adopting a standard approach provides an unambiguous means of communicating aspects of the design to those who be implementing the system.

The overall design will be judged against a set of criteria which can vary dramatically between establishments, but will typically contain:

* Cost of implementation and operation.

* Reliability of hardware and software components.

* Accuracy to which the results must be achieved.

* Security of the data.

* Flexibilty of the design to varying applications.

* Integration with existing or proposed systems.

* Expansibilty for other projects.

* Acceptability on the part of the user and management.

1.3.6 SYSTEM IMPLEMENTATION

This is another very complex stage which involves many tasks, some of which can be performed in sequence others in parallel. Typically the tasks include:

* Software specification - during which the software component is broken down into a number of modules.

* Software development - where the detailed analysis of the algorithms is performed, code is written and tested.

* System testing - test data is collected in readiness for the thorough testing of all the individual components as well as the testing of the integral system, in accordance with the testing strategy outlined in the system specification.

* Training - a comprehensive training schedule has to be formulated so that the user can adequately handle the system and be able to interpret the results/errors.

* Hardware and environmental preparation - clearly there are the

hardware specification and development stages prior to the system integration testing stage. However there is the additional aspect here of ensuring that adequate environmental preparation is performed prior to the installation of the equipment.

* Hand over - having completed all of the above stages it is finally time to hand over the system to the customer. Usually there is an overlapping period when both operational and development staff work side by side, as part of the training and commissioning sequence. It is also worth noting that in some circumstances the newly developed system has to work alongside an existing system, until sufficient experience of using the new system has been acquired.

* Documentation - in all areas the reliance upon written documentation is paramount. Written evidence regarding what has gone on before is essential when you consider how massive the development programme is, the turnover rate of staff (i.e. the number of staff leaving per month) and the timescales of the whole project. Because of these the documentation of the various stages should be done in parallel with them.

It is worth noting that throughout this stage regular design reviews are held by management to ensure that the requirements as specified by the customer are wholly satisfied.

1.3.7 SYSTEM MAINTENANCE

Software will need maintenance as well as the hardware, but in a different way (i.e. there are no parts to oil or clean). Software maintenance is required because:

* the system fails to meet the original requirements, either because there is a fault in the design or a flaw in the implementation. Such failures are not found until the system is operational.

* although the system meets its original requirements specification, experience has shown that its performance could be improved by tuning various components (i.e. varying system parameters).

* as a result in changes in the operational environment the original requirements specification is no longer valid.

Clearly documentation is important. The old documentation is needed to effect change properly and new documentation is required to reflect what changes have been made, and why. Eventually the system as developed will be shown to be obsolete and require replacement, either for economic, technical or organisational reasons. The project life cycle has gone full circle.

Having obtained a picture of the overall issues surrounding project development in the real world we now need to turn our attention to the problems
associated with software development.

During the past decade many people within the computer industry began to
recognise circumstances which have since been collectively labelled 'the
software crisis' - the overriding aspect of which was that software costs
escalated dramatically so as to become the largest expenditure item in
many computer-based systems. The main features were identified as:

* the existence of few, or no, guidelines on which to base effective
  control procedures

* schedules and completion dates were rarely kept

* as software systems grew the quality of finished products became
  suspect.

The difficulties were actually rooted in the new problems associated with
the management of a project which produced something that was really very
different - an intangible called software. Can you imagine how frustrating
it was for management when their questions produced excuses in the form of
technical jargon which they were unable to understand? Even in situations
where they did understand the technical jargon they wouldn't have suffient
confidence to query a, supposedly, computing expert. A more disciplined
approach, susceptible to project management, was essential.

1.4   The Birth of Software Engineering

In response to the software crisis a set of techniques evolved, called
software engineering. These techiques deal with software as an engineering
product that requires specification, design, implementation, testing and
maintenance, the engineering principles required for the development of
these systems encompassing both technical and non-technical aspects.

The project life-cycle shown earlier had a clearly defined schedule with a
natural flow and a relatively successful conclusion. In practice it has
not. It consists of highly complex interactions and parallel developments
no matter how hard the theoreticians try and formalise the process.

Those involved with the development and usage of software have identified
the stages of what has been termed, the software life-cycle. These are
shown in Figure 1.3, and described briefly in what follows. As might be
expected, in many ways these stages reflect the functions performed in
their project life-cycle counterpart.

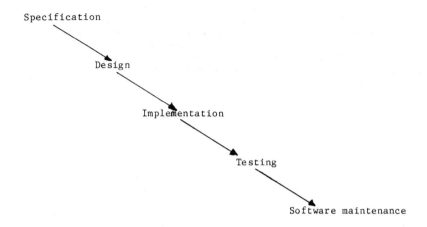

Fig 1.3   Software Life-cycle

1.4.1 SPECIFICATION

This is the part of the life-cycle which is concerned with the formulation of a software requirements specification in terms of its functions and operational constraints. The requirements also included is information about the external system behaviour and any necessary support environments. Particular attention must be given to the hardware on which the software is to perform, so as to highlight aspects that may cause problems at a later date.

1.4.2 DESIGN

A software design must be derived from an analysis of the software requirements. At this stage a suitable design notation/methodology is adopted both as a means of assistance and a gauge by which alternative solutions may be assessed. Such techniques would be used to produce a good design, which is the platform upon which 'good' software is built.

1.4.3 IMPLEMENTATION

This stage of the development deals with the realisation of code on the target system. This programming activity is dependent upon individual skill, attention to detail, knowledge of how best to use the available tools, and a management organisation that is prepared to accept the value of a good programmer (not necessarily in monetary terms).

1.4.4 TESTING

Validation is a continuing process through each stage of the software life-cycle. Testing is that part of the validation process which is normally carried out when implementation is complete. Testing involves:

* exercising the program using data which is similar to the real data on which the real program is designed to execute

* observing the outputs

* inferring program errors or inadequacies from anomalies in that output

This can only be achieved through the establishment of a suitable design strategy which not only tests to see if the individual components meet their requirements, but to ensure that the integrated system functions correctly.

1.4.5 SOFTWARE MAINTENANCE

Upon completion of the implementation stage the produced software is handed over to the operations staff, at which point the software life-cycle traditionally enters its most expensive stage: maintenance. Problems associated with software maintenance can invariably be traced to deficiences in the way the software was designed and developed. A lack of control and discipline in the early stages of the software life-cycle nearly always translates into problems in the last stage.

1.5 Summary

* Software engineering is not simply the business of writing a program.

* Although the act of writing a program can be straightforward, it can be an awesome experience if it is not done in a well structured, disciplined, and controlled fashion from the outset.

* In industry, software production is usually only one aspect of a complex project development sequence which encompasses such aspects as training, parallel hardware development, individual module and integration testing and customer acceptance.

* There are influences outside the software engineer's control which can seriously affect the production of good software; these cannot be satisfactorily simulated in an educational environment.

* The dependency upon documentation is self-evident when one considers the consequences on project development resulting from: the alteration of either the hardware or software design specifications (or both), staff leaving, the importance of integration testing, customer acceptance and maintenance.

1.6   Things to Think About

* Try to imagine the effect it would have on software production if, during the development stage, the hardware specification was altered.

* Given the above and assuming that adequate funding has been provided to redesign parts of the software, what would be the consequences of not having adequate documentation?

* What would be the affect if at the half-way stage of the development of a software product 50%, say, of the programming personnel suddenly left to start up their own competitive company?

* If project X was successfully produced in one language and another customer wanted an identical product, Y, in another language, what documentation would be required?

* What problems do you think there are associated with the development of software for a distributed computing system, geographically distributed over tens of miles?

CHAPTER TWO

The Need for Documentation

"Documentation is like sex: when it's good, it's terrific;
when it's bad, well ... it's still better than nothing."

Anon

2.1 Introduction

Or, to put it another way, be grateful that you're getting any at all.

A complete computer system will comprise hardware, software and documentation - each has their role to play.And yet, whereas no customer would
knowingly accept defective hardware, or a program that doesn't meet its
specification, inadequate documentation has always been tolerated. The
reasons for this are rooted in computing history.

For many years computer systems users were also computer systems
producers. That is, those who were trying to use documentation generated
by another manufacturer appreciated the difficulties involved because they
were also in the business of producing documentation themselves. A
tolerance born of mutual commiseration became the norm.

Slowly, however, the position is changing, and two factors in particular
can be cited. Firstly, the accelerating growth of numbers of 'simple'
computer users: businesses, for instance, with no expert computing staff,
who purchase a system to do a particular job of work. For them, the
documentation is the source of all knowledge: it has to answer all the
questions. The growth of the home computer market has exerted similar
pressures on the myriad software houses in a remarkable show of history
repeating itself within a short space of time.

The second factor is that of the software crisis discussed in Chapter 1. Complex systems generate complex errors; errors can only be solved quickly if the original source code is adequately documented. A lack of documentation - or worse, documentation that is out of date - will mean that a lengthy period of investigation has to be undertaken before a programmer can even begin to tackle the problem.

Documentation, and good documentation at that, is essential therefore. The fact remains however, that people who enjoy producing documentation are few and far between (technical authorship, as a result, is a well-paid profession). The reasons might be summarised as follows:

* Writing is extremely hard work;

* Technical writing is more a matter of report than creation - there is little or no scope for flights of fancy, jokes or even quotations to relieve the tedium;

* Documentation has to be totally accurate, which imposes the need not only to write, but to check and re-check before rewriting.

Many software producers do not employ technical authors, however. They expect their analysts and programmers, people perhaps quite unsuited to the task, to act as documentors. This inevitably means that the job is left until the exciting bits of systems analysis, programming and testing have been done. Since the next, even more, exciting project is by then on the horizon, can it be any wonder that much documentation ends up as a sketchy afterthought cobbled together under sufferance.

This is completely wrong of course. By the time the end of the project is reached the only documenting activity that should be taking place is that of tidying up, of t-crossing and i-dotting the collection of documents that have been produced throughout the whole development of the software system.

In this chapter, then, we will be concerned primarily with looking at what documentation needs to be produced, and at what point in the project life-cycle this should happen. Before doing so, however, it is necessary to spend a little time on definitions.

2.2 Types of Documentation

The word 'documentation' is an umbrella term employed to describe the sum total of the written information concerning the outcome of a software development project. Under this umbrella, however, will be sheltering information which is markedly different - in what it sets out to achieve, in its intended audience, in its content and style. In order that the full role of documentation can be appreciated, therefore, it is important to distinguish between different types of document; and, more importantly, to be clear about why they are different.

Any document forming part of the sum total of documents for a particular project will fit into one of the following classes:

* specification
* plan
* description
* report

We consider the role of each in turn.

2.2.1 SPECIFICATION - "a precise, definite statement"

The specification must be just that: a precise statement of what is to be done - what, if you like, is the destination of the journey about to begin. Clearly, and unambiguously, a specification document must define; it forms the source document for that element of the project with which it deals.

There may be more than one level of specification document. The total number will relate to the size of the project, and the manner in which it is divided into smaller modules. Each level however, from the general through to the detailed, will need to be the subject of a specification.

2.2.2 PLAN - "to arrange beforehand"

The perils of developing software in an ad hoc fashion were detailed in Chapter 1. In many ways the approach can be compared to travelling without a map book, compass or schedule: it may be an enjoyable adventure to begin with, but the enjoyment tends to pall after a while - especially when one discovers that the destination is still as far away as ever.

Planning documents define how a particular aspect of the project is to be conducted. By definition, plans are produced before work begins! Major areas to be planned are those of program development, program testing and configuration control.

2.2.3 DESCRIPTION - "a representation of the features"

A specification says what is to be done, and a description details how it has been achieved: the route that was followed.

Descriptions are complementary to specifications. They deal with the same material, but from a different perspective. If you like, the specification is the 'outside' view of the software - the view of the user - whereas a description is concerned with the inside view, the detail of what actually produces the results that the user sees.

Program and data structure designs are, therefore, primary subjects for description documents.

A special case in this respect is what is generally known as The User Manual - sometimes subdivided into two volumes headed User and Operations. (As an aside, the User Manual is sometimes referred to as 'The Documentation' for a software system, as if it were the only written information available. It has to be admitted, however, that this is all too often the situation.) In actual fact, User and Operations manuals are a subset of the description documents, dealing specifically with one narrow viewpoint of the developed software.

2.2.4 REPORT - "an account of proceedings"

Reports are concerned with events, with giving an account of significant stages in the development cycle - at the traffic lights we took a wrong turn and had to go back again.

A report should thus be complementary to a plan, giving an appraisal of what happened against what was expected to happen. The major area of reporting is, not surprisingly, that of testing.

* * * * *

Specification, Plan, Description and Report are the four document classes that will be referred to throughout this book. The essential point about them is that each aims to present information in a particular way. If a document leaves its reader uncertain about which classification applies to it, then that document has been badly written.

Note, finally, that these classes are independent of the literary means being used to present the information: tables, diagrams, listings, store maps - all may form part of a particular document, but they should not be thought of a document classes in themselves.

2.3   Documentation throughout the Life-cycle

The project life-cycle described in Chapter 1 will now serve as the basis for a summary of the different documents that need to be produced during the development of a project. The key word is DURING. Not at the end, or when the muse strikes. At any point during the cycle, the state of play should be instantly discernible from the documentation that exists. The following list serves to identify the elements cf a fully documented system, and describes briefly the function and content of each document;

subsequent chapters will expand on this information. Note that the list should be regarded as representative - that is, it is exhausting but not exhaustive.

2.3.1 SYSTEM REQUIREMENTS

2.3.1.1 System Requirements Specification

This document, or collection of documents, defines the functions to be performed by the SYSTEM: that is, by the combination of hardware, software and liveware. Of particular concern will be the interfaces between the three elements - specifications such as "if the operator does this, then the software must react so as to cause the hardware to do that."

The system specification will thus also provide details of normal and peak workloads (e.g. frequencies of interactions, data rates and volumes) that the system will be required to cope with, and also of the desired level of performance in the face of such workloads. It might also cover such niceties as operating environments, reliabilty, and diagnostic facilities.

2.3.1.2 Software Requirements Specification

This might be best thought of as an amplification of the software part of the system requirements specification (with, for purely software projects such as the development of an embedded system, the system and software requirements specifications merging into one document.)

2.3.1.3 Software Development Plan

An essentially managerial document which delineates the responsibilities of each member, or group, involved with the project, including control responsibility i.e. who reports to who, and how often.

It will define schedules and timescales, and be concerned with the nasty business of budgets: estimates of how much manpower the job will require and when, what hardware resources are needed, and - most difficult of all - how long the project will take to complete.

The plan also lays down the standards (if any) which must be followed, e.g. approved programming languages and software development tools, design methodologies, or even documentation standards.

2.3.1.4 Test Strategy Plan

Testing? As part of systems requirements? A bit early to be thinking about testing isn't it? Surely that comes along later, when there's been some development? Not so. From the earliest stage it is necessary for there to be a clear idea about the nature and level of testing to which the software is to be subjected during its development. This is detailed by the Test Strategy Plan.

As its name suggests, it is a document which is concerned not so much with the details of actual tests - these do not have to be sorted out until rather nearer the time - but with the approach that is to be taken. For instance, will a simulation system have to be produced for testing purposes: it is a bit difficult to test the software which controls the landing of an aircraft, for instance, in any other way.

What are the general acceptance criteria? What is the procedure to be followed in the event of a test failure? What constututes the failure of a test anyway? Are there any aspects of the system which are untestable and, if so, have these been clearly stated? By having such a guideline available, the systems developers know from the outset what is expected of the product on which they, and their reputations, are to be judged.

2.3.1.5 Configuration Management Plan

The elements of a software system - documentation as well as programs and data - must be subjected to rigorous control in order that consistency is maintained amongst the many aspects of the project. For instance, it is essential that the existence of multiple versions of a program module are controlled in such a way as to prevent the accidental use of an old version in a supposedly up-to-date program.

Documentation should be subject to similar controls, ensuring that program changes caused by the discovery of errors are reflected by corresponding alterations in the appropriate documents; and, what is more, that the amendments are made. A configuration management plan lays down the procedures for implementing such safeguards.

2.3.1.6 Quality Assurance Plan

This document details the manner in which a continual assessment will be made of the adherence, in practice, of the project development to the other plans cited above. Thus it is primarily concerned with the laying down of procedures concerned with ensuring that questions such as the following may be answered:

* Is the agreed design methodology being used?
* Are review meetings taking place, and being conducted correctly?
* Are programming standards being adhered to?

* Are tests being conducted correctly, and the results recorded?
* Do the test results indicate compliance with requirements?
* Is documentation being produced?

2.3.2 SYSTEMS DESIGN AND SPECIFICATION

2.3.2.1 Software Design Specification

The software requirements specification now acts as the starting point for what may be a whole series of complementary software design specification documents. Obviously the complexity of the task will determine exactly how many different documents will have to be produced; in general, however, we may assume that there will be a 'top-level' design specification together with a number of subordinate design specifications which go into more detail.

An outline specification of the software design will define the structure of the software system to be developed, relating it at all times to the requirements specification. In this respect three major areas have to be covered:

* Identification of program modules, and their individual functions;

* Identification of necessary interrelationships between these modules, and a definition of the manner in which any such interactions will be achieved;

* Identification of data structures to be employed by the software package, their basic design and a definition of the rules by which these data structures are to be accessed and manipulated by the modules.

2.3.2.2 Detailed Software Design Specifications

No surprises here. It is a case of taking each of the modules that have been specified in the Outline Software Design Specification document and subjecting them to a further refinement into program units. Where complexity demands it, these detailed specifications might lead to a number of levels of refinement, effectively making the final design documentation into a hierarchical collection of smaller documents.

Ultimately the products of this phase will be used as the working designs for program writing. If the design is incorrect, then the program won't work either; as important, if not more so, is that both program and design documents will have to be changed, requiring additional effort. Thus it is the design stage - not the programming stage - which it is crucial to get right. It must be expected, therefore, that the documents comprising the specification of software design details will, and should, undergo considerable review and change.

2.3.2.3 Data Structure Design Specifications

Software exists to manipulate data; specifications for data design must therefore be prepared with just as much care as program designs. The data structure design specification will be concerned with the full spectrum of data handling as identified in the software requirements specification. For instance:

Input: * What information is provided by the system user?
* Will any data formats be imposed?
* Are any data items to be accorded default values?

Processing: * What files are needed? How are they to be organised in terms of indexes, records, chaining and so on?
* What data structuring features does the programming language possess, and how should they be used?
* What rules have to be followed when passing data between program modules and units; is there any case for shared data?

Output: * What data has to be output, and to what medium?
* Does it have to be converted into a special form for display?
* Will files be created for future use? If so, what will be their structure?

Note that there will normally be some overlap between a Data Structure Design Specification and the various Software Design documents; data flow considerations, for instance, will figure in both. This should not be regarded as duplication however. As has been stressed elsewhere, it is quite proper for separate documents to cover the same aspect of the software design from a different angle. In this instance, views of the way in which the system data is being organised, and the ways in which it is to be processed should be complementary.

2.3.2.4 Test Specifications

Although not immediately obvious, the content of a Test Specification document will lead on from both the Software Requirements Specification and Software Design Specification documents.

Firstly the Test Specification will define the tests that are to be conducted on individual modules and units. Naturally these will be influenced by the software requirements - we want to know that the software does what it is supposed to do. But this might only apply when a number of units/ modules have been glued together: the design of the software determines

25

this. Testing should not be left until this stage, but conducted on each
and every component. Thus it is that the ultimate design, which defines
program units and modules, effectively dictates the elements which have to
be put under the microscope; the Test Specification says what those tests
will be.

From this it should be apparent that another area of testing has to be
carried out: integration testing. That is, verification that two or more
modules/units, which work on their own, combine to form a larger program
item which also works. Here then, the Test Specification document will
define the tests to be carried out in each instance of integration.

2.3.3 SOFTWARE DEVELOPMENT

2.3.3.1 Module and Unit Design Descriptions

The progression from design to implementation is reflected in the
documents that are produced at this stage. Our concern now is that of
describing accurately what has been done in an attempt to fully implement
the design: practice as opposed to theory. This is not to say, of course,
that the two documents will be differ wildly - at least not if the design
task has been done well. But there may be variations, and it is certainly
one of the functions of design descriptions to point to such areas.

One other vital point is this: that the design descriptions will be the
starting point for any maintenance work that has to be done in the future
- as it certainly will. Errors will be uncovered as and when the system is
used in anger (not literally, one hopes) possibly months or even years
after development. High quality design descriptions will considerably
ease the whole business of software maintenance; inadequate documentation
at this level will turn the whole task into a veritable nightmare.

A description, then, has to present the facts of implementation in a way
that leaves out no relevant detail, but does not confuse. If the software
has been well structured this task is possible, with each module/unit
being described independently so as to mirror the design specification
series of documents.

The heart of each document will be the module/unit code. This will be
related to the original specifications so that, for instance, the description of the role played by different variables, arrays and files refers
to the pertinent parts of the document on Data Structure Design; or that
the use of segments/procedures and their interconnections is consistent
with that laid down in the Module/Unit Design Specification.

Because we are dealing with code at this level of documentation, much of
the work should already have been done through the medium of program
comments. A listing is, of course, a valuable part of the software documentation; the important thing to realise is that it is but a part, not THE
documentation. Other computer-generated information plays a part at this
stage. Cross-reference listings, memory maps, load maps - all describe the
software implementation from the inside.

2.3.3.2 User and Operations Manuals

Unless it is completely embedded, the software system also has to be described from the outside as it were: the actual implementation has to be detailed for the potential user(s) of the system.

A User Manual is peculiar in that it is part of the descriptive set of documents, but also needs to stand as a self-contained item in way that no other single document has. For this reason it tends to be a composite document, containing bits of the requirements and design specifications as well as giving implementation details of relevance to the user. It must serve as both an introductory, and a reference, document - objectives that are often sufficiently incompatible for the decision to be taken that two volumes of user documentation should be produced. There is another consideration also. If any document is to be read by a non-computing person, it is the User Manual. All the others, although needing to be no less well-written, can at least assume some level of technical expertise on the part of their reader. To write for a novice user, on a subject like computing which has a jargon-rating approaching that of the medical profession, in a way that is readable and yet conveys the necessary information, is no mean achievement. The computer rooms of the world are littered with the efforts of those software developers who have tried and failed.

If the system is large enough to require a 'third party' to carry out the duties of an operator then an Operations Manual will also be needed. This document will only deal superficially with the actual functions being performed by the software. Rather it will be concerned with describing the steps involved in initiating the system - and closing it down, if special actions need to be taken. Most importantly the Operations Manual will have to cover, to the point of pedantry sometimes, how the operator must react to error situations or any special conditions that may be presented whilst the software is in action.

2.3.4 TEST AND ACCEPTANCE

2.3.4.1 Test Reports

The execution of any significant test should cause a Test report to be produced. What constitutes a 'significant test'? A test conducted in accordance with the Test Plan, and defined in a Test Specification.

Thus a Test Report, or Reports if the tests have to be repeated again for some reason, effectively rounds off the plan/specify/ execute cycle for the testing of a particular module or program unit. The actual nature of such tests will be discussed later; at this point, however, suffice it to say that they could take the form of anything from a fully programmed test with simulated data through to a simple manual code inspection. Whatever the case, the result is a Test Report which may in practice turn out to be no more than a single page addendum to the Test Plan.

Note particularly that, if the test produces satisfactory results, then the Test Report is a concluding document. If, however, the test fails, then the Report assumes the status of an initiating document: it will certainly cause a change to any relevant design description documents, and could cause changes to be made in design specifications if the fault has been caused through poor design rather than faulty implementation.

2.3.4.2 Acceptance Reports

At the end of the day, the complete software package has to be presented for final acceptance - or rejection - by 'the customer'. The package should comprise both the software AND its associated documentation. A customer prepared to accept the former without passing judgement is unwise; a customer who intends either to maintain, or pay some third party to maintain, the software post-delivery and still fails to subject the documentation to some acceptance criteria is a fool.

Ideally, the Acceptance Report will be a perfect complement to the original Software Requirements Specification: it will state that every-thing that was required has been supplied. In practice, however, this may well not be the case. Some of the requirements may have proved impossible to implement; some may have changed to reflect a later development; some - perhaps in the area of systems performance - may be lacking, but are to be the subject of agreed further work post-delivery. Thus the Acceptance Report is just that: a statement of what has been accepted, comprising details of both conformance to the original requirements and discrepancy details of those areas in which the requirement has not been met.

2.4   Documentation Quality

It is an unfortunate fact that the quality of software documentation, or rather the lack of quality, only becomes fully apparent in times of maximum embarrassment. When the user/operator needs to discover a fact quickly to recover from some emergency, or when a hitherto low-down bug has crawled to the surface and has to be fixed immediately, that is when the inadequacies of the documentation are revealed.

It is therefore important to subject the documentation to some sort of acceptance criteria. As far as they can be such criteria must be object-ive, and not of the subjective 'It is essential that diagrams are clearly presented, preferably in red and black (which looks very nice)' sort. For what it is worth, there now follows a brief check-list of qualities; should each be met, then you have a very good set of software document-ation indeed.

Positive qualities first. Documents should be -

* CHANGEABLE - changes affecting one document will almost certainly mean
  changes to many others; the 'changeability' of a document is a reflec-
  tion of the ease with which all affected parts of the documentation
  may be located.

* COMPLETE - a document is complete if it contains exactly that information which is relevant to its use: no less, of course, but no more
  either, since this would indicate redundant detail.

* COMPREHENSIBLE - if the information can be readily understood by each
  member of the intended reader group, assuming average levels of pre-
  requisite knowledge of course, then the document can be considered
  comprehensible.

* CONFORMANT - documents should fully conform to whatever standards have
  been laid down for their production.

* IDENTIFIED - identification is the suitability of a document, or more
  likely a collection of documents, to be used in production of answers
  to an open question.

* UP-TO-DATE - self-evident. A document should reflect, at all times,
  the current status of that which it aims to describe. It is a fact of
  life that most documents are in a permanent state of soon-to-be-
  updatedness.

Finally some negatives. Documents should NOT be -

* AMBIGUOUS - that is, the same document, read by two different people,
  should leave both with an identical understanding of the subject in
  question. If this is not so, then the document is ambiguous. This is
  almost impossible to achieve if the document is written in English -
  such are the riches of our language!

* CONTRADICTORY - A document which (unambiguously!) makes conflicting
  statements about the same topic is contradictory. No reader of a document should be left to guess at, or conduct research into, what the
  software actually does.

2.5 Summary

* A software system must be considered incomplete unless a complete set
  of related documentation has also been produced.

* It is possible to place any document in one of only four classes:
  specification, plan, description or report. If this is not so, then
  the document has been poorly written.

* A fully documented system will comprise documents relating to every

phase of the software life-cycle. Thus documentation is itself an activity which takes place throughout the duration of the project, not as the final phase prior to completion.

* Quality applies as much to documentation as it does to software; quality criteria can be defined.

2.6   Things to Think About

Put yourself in the position of Baron Frankenstein, and consider the creation of your monster (or prototype intelligent robot if you wish) as a software development project:

* For one part of the monster's anatomy, try to define the role - and target readership - of documents for specification, plan, description and report.

* Consider the range of documents needed to cover the monster's development throughout the project (pardon the pun) life-cycle.

CHAPTER THREE

The Requirements Specification

3 THE REQUIREMENTS SPECIFICATION

> "O! what men dare do! what men may do! what men
> daily do, not knowing what they do!"
>
> Shakespeare: Much Ado About Nothing IV.i.[19]

3.1   The Purpose of a Requirements Specification

It may turn out that the advent of electronic mail will have an effect unforseen by its designers: a national shortage of old envelopes. If this does prove to be the case, the whole process of software development will be forced into making a quite radical decision - what are requirements specifications to be written on now?

With luck the answer will be something rather more suited to what is arguably the most important part of the software life-cycle: the production of a comprehensive statement about just what is expected of a computer system - a requirements specification.

We will shortly consider the content of an example requirements specification. It will be seen that its production, even for a smallish program, is not a trivial matter, involving an investment of no small measure of effort. Before doing so, therefore, it seems sensible to offer some answers to the primordial student question: "why bother?"

* At some point, the requirement has to be specified - even if it only amounts to the programmer needing to decide what to do next. If the requirement cannot be specified, then it cannot be implemented. In crude terms, it is better to specify first and then implement after, since recognition of an insoluble problem at the outset can save an awful lot of time and money.

* All subsequent phases of the project development life-cycle lead on

from this point - or, more meaningfully perhaps, look back at what the requirements specification said. The more accurately the requirement can be specified, therefore, the less trouble incurred in the future.

*   If requirements specification and system implementation are not being performed by the same party, then some form of written communication between the two is essential. This will invariably be the case, whether the parties belong to the same department or company or - as is most likely in the real world - they are in the roles of customer and supplier (e.g. with a government contract). In this respect, the requirements specification is able to form the basis of an invitation to tender. Although a supplier's response may lead to changes in the specification, it is essential that the customer puts into writing his own perception of what is wanted. (In practice this exercise may often be conducted in conjunction with the likely contractor - the point still applies, however).

*   When finally agreed between supplier and customer, the requirements specification can become the first agreed (baseline) document for the project.

Having accepted the desirability of producing a requirements specification as the first step in the project, it is necessary to define the boundaries of such a document. Our concern is to specify what the proposed system is required to achieve - in many cases, this being virtually the same as saying how the system will look to its eventual user. The operative word is 'what'.

The requirements specification is not a system design document. It is not concerned with details of implementation (other than at the relatively superficial level of the division of labour between hardware, software and operator) but with stating clearly and concisely what is to be implemented - it is a specification from which systems design proceeds.

3.2   The Content of a Requirements Specification

Within the inevitable constraints imposed by chapter length, we shall endeavour to illustrate the basic form of a requirements specification by developing an example from scratch, or thereabouts. The following is our starting point:

> A SYSTEM THAT WILL ALLOW THE STORAGE AND RETRIEVAL OF NAMES
> AND TELEPHONE NUMBERS.

The student might recognise this as being of similar length to programming coursework specifications. As a requirements specification, the only thing that can be said in its favour is that it would definitely fit onto the back of an old envelope.

* * * * *

The only real rule governing the content of a requirements specification is that it should cover everything, clearly and unambiguously. Such aspects as layout, division into sections and sub-sections, use of cross-reference and indexing techniques - these are subordinate. Various different styles could be adopted (see Bibliography, especially IEE (1985)); the outline given below is just one of many that could do the job satisfactorily.

In general terms a requirements specification will comprise 6 sections, as follows:

Function : A 'user-eye' view of the system, dealing with all aspects of the user interface.

Allocation : Delineation of responsibility, for each of the functions that have been defined, to hardware/software/operator.

Constraints: Any particular limitations on the way the system is to do its work, together with their level of importance.

Standards : A definition of existing - that is, known and documented - techniques which have to be applied to the development of the system.

Quality : Details of the quality control procedures under which the the project's progress will monitored and controlled.

Schedule : Targets - what is expected to be ready by when.

We now consider each of these sections in turn, applying them so as to develop a requirements specification our computerised telephone directory system.

3.2.1 FUNCTION

A specification of each system function is provided in this section. Here the customer - the future user of the system - should be able to see clear confirmation that his/her requirements have been understood; the designer of the system should be left in no doubt about what is to be implemented at the next stage.

In general terms the following aspects will need to be covered. It should be noted that although one blanket statement will often suffice, this information will need to be supplied for EACH function.

(a) The type of information that will be provided to the system, and the input medium to be used (e.g. keyboard, document, signal).

(b) The system's action on the information it has received, i.e. details of the 'processing' to be carried out. Where applicable this could include such things as, e.g. minimum lengths for character items and degree of accuracy for numeric calculations.

(c) The type of information that has to be output by the system, and the output medium to be used (e.g. screen display, document, signal).

(d) What the system must prevent (e.g. acceptance of invalid information, unauthorised access), and the manner in which the detection of such conditions has to be reported (e.g. error message, audible warning, self-destruct).

(e) The loads that the system must be able accommodate, usually in terms of average and worst cases (e.g. frequencies of data arrival, volumes of data required on-line).

(f) The speed with which the system is required to perform the stated functions (e.g. response time at a terminal, execution time for a program)

(g) Possible requirements for reconfigurations or expansions (e.g. changes in locations or numbers of terminals);

(h) An indication of required system availability (e.g. continuously available, never on a Sunday), together with standards of reliability required (e.g. extent of degredation or loss of service, frequency and duration of failures acceptable),

(i) Requirements for acceptance of the completed system (to be stated explicitly, even though they may be implied by the above).

Let us illustrate this contents list for the functional specification by returning to our opening-shot requirement:

A SYSTEM THAT WILL ALLOW THE STORAGE AND RETRIEVAL OF NAMES
AND TELEPHONE NUMBERS.

An introductory paragraph to the function section is necessary to set the scene and thus, whilst the above is totally unacceptable as a requirements specification, it could become our 'abstract' if expanded as follows:

A SINGLE-USER, DISC-BASED TELEPHONE DIRECTORY SYSTEM THAT
WILL SUPPORT THE STORAGE AND RETRIEVAL OF NAMES AND TELE-
PHONE NUMBERS. THREE MAJOR FUNCTIONS ARE TO BE OFFERED:
ADDITION OF NEW ITEMS TO THE DIRECTORY, MODIFICATION OF
EXISTING ITEMS, AND SEARCHING THROUGH THE DIRECTORY FOR A
GIVEN ITEM. FULL DATA VALIDATION AND ERROR HANDLING MECH-
ANISMS ARE TO BE INCORPORATED.

Now to consider the contents, grouped under the entries (a) to (i) defined above:

(a) Input Medium

* The input medium to be used for all functions is to be a keyboard.

Information to be input

* Information will need to be provided to the system by the user as
  follows:

  ADD   : name and telephone number;
  MODIFY: name or telephone number of entry to be modified, followed
          by details of the changes to be made;
  SEARCH: name or telephone number for which a search is to be made.

(b) Processing

* Data input is to be validated before further action is taken, with the
  user informed in the event of an invalid data input. Thereafter:

  ADD   : a combined name/telephone number record is to be added to the
          database;
  MODIFY: following input of a revised data item, the modified name/
          telephone number record is added to the database with the
          original record being deleted;
  SEARCH: the database is searched for the required item, the complete
          name/telephone number record being retrieved.

  Accuracy

* All string comparisons are to be made using the full data item as
  input by the user. A comparison is to be deemed successful if this
  string matches with the characters of the stored item.

(c) Output Medium

* The output medium to be used for all functions is to be either a
  screen or printer.

  Information to be output

* Information will need to be output by the system to the user as
  follows:

  ADD   : an indication that the function has been successfully carried
          out.
  MODIFY: an indication that the original record has been successfully
          modified, together with confirmation of the content of the
          modified record.
  SEARCH: name and telephone number from each record matched against
          the supplied search string. If the output medium is a screen,
          then a user control must be supplied to enable single-step
          output.

(d) Detection of system errors

* All errors caused by malfunctioning of either the hardware or the resident support software [e.g. operating system] shall be detected, and

35

reported to the user.

* Failures during the transfer of data to/from disc must automatically
  cause the data transfer to be retried; an error indication should be
  be produced only after repeated failure. In all cases the integrity of
  the database must be maintained. A warning should be provided in the
  event of the database becoming 75% full.

Detection of user errors

* The following errors should be detected and reported to the user by
  means of an error message. Correction of an erroneous condition by the
  user should not normally require the re-input of valid data.

  ADD   : * attempted omission of either name or telephone number;
           * failure to add new item because database is full.
  MODIFY: * attempted omission of data item for search;
           * failure to find nominated data item in the database;
           * attempted omission of either name or telephone number on
             input of the required modification.
  SEARCH: * attempted omission of data item for search;
           * failure to find nominated data item in the database.

* It should be possible for the user to abandon any function mid-stream,
  with the integrity of the database being maintained.

                        * * * * * *

So far, so good. Before continuing however, let us refer back to the revised 'abstract' suggested as a preface to the Function section of this
requirements specification. It mentioned, deliberately:

    A SINGLE-USER ...   TELEPHONE DIRECTORY SYSTEM ..

How, if at all, would things need to differ if the specification was for a
MULTI-USER system? If, for instance, we were looking at a system to be
used by the 'Directory Enquiries' branch of a national telephone service?

Well, for a system of very limited functionality, sections (a) to (d) of
our example could apply equally well to a multi-user or single-user
system. Apart from additional subsections throughout to specify the role
of a master console - to which all system error messages would be directed, for instance - the view given is that to be received by any
individual user, and the fact that there may be many such users who
receive the same view is of little consequence.

However, this cannot be said as we consider remaining sections (e) to (i).
The content here will be heavily dependent on the expected levels of
concurrent usage to which the system will be put. For this reason, the
examples will not just deal with the 'simple' requirement used up until
now, but try also to indicate how the requirements specification would
need to be extended to deal with something rather more complex. Comments
in square brackets [] are included where necessary to provide additional
explanation.

Note also that where a numeric value would appear in the requirements specification the indication ..x.. is used, since even with this simple example the range of possibilities is large. (A home user, for instance, might be expected to specify a need to hold a relatively small amount of data - but the odd one could be looking to automate finger-walking through a complete issue of Yellow Pages). Suffice it to say that a value of suitable magnitude would have to be determined for the purposes of specification.

* * * * * *

(e) System loading

* The system must be able to support up to ..x.. terminals. [multi-user]

* The system must be able to hold ..x.. name/telephone number records on-line.

* During any one-hour period of operation there will need to be carried out a total of:

    ..xx.. (average), ..x.. (peak) ADD functions
    ..xx.. (average), ..x.. (peak) MODIFY functions
    ..xx.. (average), ..x.. (peak) SEARCH functions

    [for a multi-user system, it would also be necessary to define the distribution of these average and peak values across the number of terminals]

(f) Performance

* Performance requirements in terms of response times for the different functions are as follows:

    ADD   function: average ..x.. seconds, maximum ..x.. seconds
    MODIFY function: average ..x.. seconds, maximum ..x.. seconds
    SEARCH function: average ..x.. seconds, maximum ..x.. seconds

* The above requirement applies to the concurrent operation of up to ..x.. terminals. [for a multi-user system]

(g) Expansion/Reconfiguration

* It is anticipated that, over the next ..x.. years, the system will need to meet the following growth requirements:

    Increase of ..x.. % in stored name/telephone numbers;
    Increase of ..x.. % in the defined per-hour function usage, uniformly
         distributed across the functions;
    Increase of ..x.. terminals in concurrent operation [multi-user].

    [The requirement could now continue in one of two ways -

EITHER:

* sufficient spare capacity in terms of main and disc storage, and processor power, must be available to accommodate an expansion of this
magnitude (figures could be given)

OR:

* it must be possible to implement such an expansion by means of an
enhancement of the system supplied to meet the original requirement]

(h) System availability

* The system is required to operate on a 24-hour, 7-day basis.

* Reliability levels must be at the level of at least ..x..% uptime over
any period of ..x.. months operation.

* Recovery from a software crash should take a maximum of ..x.. minutes.

* Archiving of the database to/from long-term storage must be possible
in parallel with normal operation.

[This would be the sort of expectation for a major system that needs
to be permanently on-line; the home user wanting to use the system in
this way could specify exactly the same requirement, of course - the
only differences are those of scale.]

(i) Acceptance

[Much of what has gone before will be repeated in this section, the
object of which is to give a formal indication of those aspects of the
requirements specification that will comprise the basis of acceptance
trials on the supposedly finished system. The general outline given
below would be supplemented by detailed statements wherever necessary]

Upon completion of the system, a 3-phase acceptance test will be used
as follows:

* Phase 1: the supplier's standard installation tests, after which it
shall be certified that the system has been installed in
accordance with the supplier's specifications.

Phase 2: the customer or customer's representative shall carry out the
system acceptance test to ensure compliance of all functional, operational and performance items of this specification.

Phase 3: The customer or customer's representative shall use the
system for ..x.. months to determine that a ..x..% uptime
figure can be maintained.

38

3.2.2 ALLOCATION

[Each of the functions defined must be allocated to the appropriate system element - hardware, software or operator. In practice the approach taken is often to consider hardware and software separately, with the tasks of the operator defined within each area as appropriate. As a consequence separate hardware and software design documents might be produced with the twain not meeting again until the stage of system integration, at which point the two have to be put together. Given that details of the inter- faces between hardware and software appear in one, and preferably both, of the documents, this approach is perfectly acceptable.]

e.g. dealing with an ADD/MODIFY/SEARCH function:

HARDWARE: * The whole database will need to be on-line whilst the system is in operation.

      * Failure of a disc access during an ADD/MODIFY/SEARCH operation must cause a software-detectable error code to enable the software to initiate corrective or recovery action, and a visible/audible warning to the operator in the event of any failure which may be rectified by operator intervention, e.g. disc drive offline

SOFTWARE: * Processing of input data and production of output is expected to be carried out by software loaded from external medium [i.e. not firmware]. However, the tasks of reading/validation of input data, and the generation of output displays, may be carried out by a combination of loaded software and (e.g. for screen control) firmware.

[One particular aspect of allocation concerns the information that the system will be holding. The requirements for data files could also be dealt with in this section, therefore, including details of any databases or data files currently in existence.]

* The system will employ a single database comprising name/telephone number records.

* This database will need to be part of the delivered system ..

    [EITHER]

    .. its content being established by input of data from the existing system of printed telephone directories. [A home-user might specify input of data from the telephone book in the hallway.]

    [OR]

    .. its content being established by transfer of data from the existing collection of ..x.. 8-inch floppy discs.

3.2.3 CONSTRAINTS

[In this section technical and managerial constraints are dealt with. Typical categories in this section would include -

    Environment - temperatures, level of humidity ..
    Resources   - required spare capacity of cpu time/memory ..
    Schedule   - deadlines, progress points ..
    Cost   - not more than ..
]

* The system must run in an office environment, [Office environment is a phrase generally understood to be synonymous with both a lack of air-conditioning and the presence of grime] and should not require any additional power supply [i.e. nothing more than a 3-pin plug]

* When the on-line database has been initialised, 50% of the available disc space should remain unused, so as to accommodate future expansion.

* The implemented system should be delivered within ..x.. months of the date of contract.

* A budget of £..x.. has been allocated for this project [i.e. if you want the job, don't ask for more than this!]

[In addition to the specification of a constraint, it is often appropriate to indicate a level of constraint as well. For instance, one might specify that a particular requirement is vital and must be met in full by the system; alternatively a somewhat looser constraint might be imposed with some relaxation possible if within stated acceptable limits]

For instance, a loosening of the second of the above four constraints:

* When the on-line database has been initialised, about 50% – and not less than 40%, - of the available disc space should remain unused, so as to accommodate future expansion.

3.2.4 STANDARDS

[A standard might be viewed as another kind of constraint - imposed, in effect, upon design and implementation. In other words, there is included within the requirements specification at this point a standards section which will lay down that, in some respect or another, the designer/systems analyst/programmer must do their job in a certain way.

Aha! you say, but how does this square with your earlier categoric insistence that the requirements specification is not a design document? Simple. The requirements specification serves to define the framework for the project; within that framework the designer et al do indeed have total freedom. A standard serves to strengthen the framework, nothing more.

For instance, a computer bureau might insist that the user documentation produced as part of the project conform to a particular defined standard. This is good sense since, in this way, the users of the bureau's computer services will appreciate the fact that the trauma of learning to use the new product is reduced by having the documentation in a familiar style.

Again, a customer may wish to specify that a computer program be written in a particular programming language. This is less desirable, since one would hope to be free to choose the most suitable language for the job, but if a customer is planning to engage in D-I-Y maintenance, or can only afford to by one particular compiler, then it makes sense to state at this stage the language to be used.

As a final point, it is not unusual to find the Standards section of the Requirements Specification to be non-existent. If the customer wishes to give the producer complete freedom of action, then this absence is quite acceptable; the important thing in such cases is that the customer knows that this freedom to decide has been given away. Our home-user is a canny individual though ..]

* All programs shall be written in Pascal, with both the source and object code being deliverable items.

3.2.5 QUALITY

[This section should cover requirements for quality control and assurance throughout the project life-cycle.

The difference here is that the requirement will be of the form "suppliers must say what they are going to do about ..", rather than "suppliers must .." In its simplest form the requirement will be that the supplier should define the Code of Practice that they will follow; to avoid the possibility of a totally general reply being received in return ("we'll do what we always do"), particular points might be put forward as needing to be specifically addressed. The following is a representative list of areas that such a response might be expected to cover:

* Project management structure, the level of expertise to be employed - how the project is going to be organised in terms of who does what, and who reports to who;

* Project planning programme - when will the different happenings take place, and in what sequence;

* Project progress control procedures - how will project development be monitored, when, and how often;

* Testing strategy and programme - what aspects of the system are to be tested, at what point in the system development cycle will the tests

take place, and what will they demonstrate;

* Quality organisation, responsibilities and procedures - whose job is it to quality assure the project, and what procedures will they be following;

* Configuration management - how will new versions of software and/or documentation be introduced and controlled so that the current status of each is always known.

We will return to the subject of Quality Assurance in Chapter 6; at this point, however, suffice it to say that the music-hall adage 'never mind the quality, feel the width' applies too often to computer systems - and it's really no joke!

Some possible statements, in addition to a request for a defined Codes of Practice, might be as follows:]

* A clear policy must be defined regarding the retesting and confirmation of all levels of software following the introduction of modifications and/or corrections.

* A programme of software design reviews must be given, and related to the expected software development cycle.

* Intermediate documentation should be defined, being the subject of, and approved output from, the stipulated design reviews.

* The test plan must include testing milestones; these must be related to the project life-cycle, and to the programme of design reviews.

3.2.6 DEVELOPMENT SCHEDULE

[A system development schedule should also form part of the requirements specification. Although, like cost, detailed schedules cannot reasonably be established without a commensurate amount of detailed hardware and software planning, general targets should be set - if only to be ridiculed by the supplier as totally impossible, not on, you must be joking mate, etc. Certainly some form of schedule will need to be agreed for contractual purposes, and the customer loses nothing by starting out with a statement of when it would be nice to see the finished product, or at least bits of it.]

* System handover is required within ..x.. months of award of contract.

3.3 Requirements Validation

En route to this point we have emphasised the obvious, but often overlooked, fact that the requirements specification is the document from which all further project development takes its lead. For this reason it should be self-evident that errors in the requirements will be propagated firstly through the design phases then, if undetected, through the coding phases; in the worst case the errors do not manifest themselves until the system has been installed and enters operation. Not unlike some of the nastier diseases, the more an error spreads throughout a system, the greater the surgery needed to remove it.

The word error as used in the above paragraph might have been written 'error', since the arguments given apply just as much to missing require- ments as to requirements that have been specified incorrectly; for a system to reach the installation stage before the customer realises that a vital feature has been overlooked is just as much a disaster as the disc- overy of a nest of bugs. Software maintenance is often more to do with the addition of forgotten features than with the correction of errors.

All of which points to the need to validate a requirements specification before it is passed to the system designer. Broadly speaking the aims of requirements validation are as follows:

* To ensure that the specification is complete. Everything that the user wants should be included, and nothing that is unwanted should be left in. This criterion is undeniably hard to achieve, since the potential of a system is often not realised until some, or all, of it has been seen in action. If an identifiable area of doubt exists then some sort of prototype system - a quick, 'how about this sort of thing' system, constructed on the strict understanding that it is to be discarded - should be considered.

  In this context, any expansion/reconfiguration section (eg 3.2.1g in the example above) would need to be looked at very carefully.

* To ensure that the specification is consistent. Requirements, although specified individually, are inevitably interrelated. Our concern here is that the eventual fulfilment of one requirement does not render the implementation of another requirement impossible because of the simple fact that the two are contradictory.

  As an admittedly extreme example, 3.2.1a above specifies that for an ADD function, a name and telephone number will be input; if the MODIFY function which follows had specified the input of the name or address of the item to be modified, the two requirements would be inconsistent - does the system hold telephone number or address, or both? To find out that the wrong information had been initialised on disc for the whole of the London telephone directory would be unfortunate.

* To ensure that the specification is realistic. Simply, there is no use including in the specification a requirement that it is not possible to implement. To ask that the SEARCH function should find a telephone number for a name that the user can't remember, for instance, would be unrealistic - at least until clairvoyant software reaches the shops.

Odd as it may seem, the cause of the biggest difficulties in carrying out the validation exercise is that our requirements document is invariably written in natural language - English, to you and me - on the premise that it can be understood by all the parties concerned. But the argument that natural language can be understood by all does not mean that the requirements document is able to be understood by all; or, worse, convey the same meaning to all those who claim to understand what has been written. A simple example will illustrate the potential for confusion:

* Two star-struck romantics dallying 'neath a silver moon might ask each other the eternal question - "What is this thing called love?"

* A rather more pragmatic couple, seeking information in their efforts to get to the bottom of things - "What is this thing called, love?"

The same words, but with a rather different response one suspects.

Natural language specification, therefore, does not always aid validation. It can introduce - as in the above example - ambiguity of meaning, with the chance that the user and the specifier, or the specifier and the designer, will interpret a statement in different ways.

In our telephone-directory system requirements example, for instance, (see 3.2.1b above) the criterion for a succesful search is given:

"All string comparisons are to be made using the full data item as input by the user. A comparison is to be deemed successful if this string matches with the characters of the stored item."

Does this mean that if our stored name is RUMPLESTILTSKIN then the only possible match is when the user inputs the 15 characters of that name? Or if the 'full data item as input by the user' is RUMP or RUMPLE will this produce a match? How about STILTS or SKIN as input data items - don't they match 'the characters of the stored item'?

Additionally, there is the inevitable affect of natural language usage causing separate elements of the requirements to be mixed together so as to blur the distinction between them. It's the 'I want you to go to the supermarket on Wednesday - oh yes, and Thursday, they have a special offer on Thursdays - and buy a couple of tons of tripe and onions' problem: what is to be bought when? A ton each day? A ton of tripe on Wednesday, with a ton of special-offer onions on Thursday? You get the picture.

Using the telephone-directory example again, an error is to be detected in the execution of the search function on (see 3.2.1d):

"attempted omission of data item for search"

But how does this square with the search criterion just mentioned:

"All string comparisons are to be made using the full data item as input by the user."

Is a null data item to be used for a search or not? The definition of what constitutes a data item should be established elsewhere, and is obviously an omission. The point to be made, though, is that in making good this omission it will be necessary to wade through the specification in order to unearth any other requirement that might be affected; all references to 'data item', 'string', 'name', 'telephone number', 'comparison', 'match' etc. would need to be examined.

Validation of requirements, therefore, becomes a major headache when those requirements are specified in natural language. A natural conclusion which is regularly reached, therefore, is that validation of requirements is a task to be avoided - which inevitably causes a bigger headache as errors surface later on in the project life-cycle. The aspirin equivalent, it is hoped, will be an eventual acceptance of formal methods of requirements specification.

Briefly, since this topic is covered more fully in Chapter 10, the aim of a 'formal method' is to develop specifications by using a narrowly-defined representation notation so as to minimise the dangers of ambiguity and/or blurring that we have identified. A variety of approaches have been, and are being, developed - variously based on some diagrammatic, programming, or mathematical notation - each with the twin objectives of ensuring that a requirements specification can be presented accurately, and proved to be presented accurately.

So, for example, we might choose to express our requirements in a form of pseudo-BASIC by firstly defining what we mean by a data item -

<data item> is_defined_as (<name> OR <telephone number>)

AND NOT <blank>

using this definition in a subsequent specification for a search -

```
SEARCH FUNCTION:

INPUT       <user data item>
IF
            <user data item> is_a <data item>
THEN
        IF
                all_characters_of <user data item> =
                start_characters_of <database item>
        THEN
                comparison_ok
        ELSE
                report_an_error
    ELSE  report_an_error
```

A notation such as this, which reduces the specification language to fewer terms that it can use (IF, THEN), each of which has a universal meaning to all readers, together with a simple rule that all other terms invented by the specifier (e.g. <data item>, all_characters_of, comparison_ok) must themselves be defined within the specification, is the essence of a formal method. Add to it the obvious potential for computer processing and the dream of a means of achieving fully validated requirements specifications comes rather closer to being realised.

3.4   Summary

*   A requirements specification is an essential starting document for a
    project, being an agreed statement between customer and supplier about
    what the software system is to do.

*   The functional part of the requirements specification will cover
    input, data processing, output, error handling, system loading, perf-
    ormance, reconfiguration, availability and acceptance.

*   The non-functional parts of the requirements specification will cover
    allocation of functions, constraints, standards, quality and develop-
    ment schedule.

*   Validation of requirements specifications should take place before any
    design work is undertaken; validation aims to show that specifications
    are complete, consistent and realistic.

*   The use of natural language for requirements specification makes auto-
    matic validation impossible; formal methods for requirements specific-
    ation are an area of current research.

3.5   Things to Think About

*   Write an outline requirements specification for a household object,

        e.g.   television
                washing machine
                spouse

*   Write a requirements specification for a microcomputer program to
    solve a set of simultaneous equations, the user being expected to type
    in the equations from the keyboard.

*   As above, but this time the equations should be taken from a disc
    file.

*   Assess each of your requirements specifications – or, better still,
    that of somebody else – against the validation criteria of complete-
    ness, consistency and realism.

*   Who should have the final say on the requirements specification – the
    customer, or the supplier?

46

CHAPTER FOUR

Data Analysis

"JUDGE: I have read your case, Mr. Smith, and I an no wiser
now than I was when I started.

SMITH: Possibly not, My Lord, but far better informed."

Earl of Birkenhead: Life of F.E.Smith

4.1   Input Data and Output Data

Not unlike a judge, a computerised system is designed to accept information about the environment or application area within which it operates,
process that acquired information and present the results of its delib-
erations to all interested parties.

Such computer systems may be thought of as comprising a collection of
functional sub-systems, each performing a pre-defined task on well-defined
items of information (or, as they are more commonly called, data items). A
simple schematic, with sub-systems for Sample, Processing and Present, is
given in Figure 4.1.

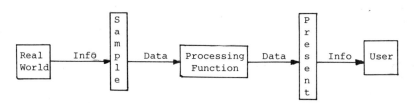

Fig. 4.1 Functional sub-system schematic

The need to sample the real world directly would be specified in the system requirement specification, and subsequently incorporated into the design of the system. The need for such 'input' requirements would be found, for example, in any control system where the objective is to monitor the state of the environment and respond to any adverse set of conditions - as in an automated central heating system, for instance, which might monitor the state of the water pressure and initiate a shut-down sequence if it were to detect that the pressure had become danger-ously high.

In performing such a task the system would automatically sample the real world conditions and convert the sampled information into a suitable format for submission to the processing sub-system. Usually such functions must be performed in real-time, thereby imposing constraints on both the software and hardware design strategies to ensure adequate response and reaction times.

There may be similar 'output' arguments regarding the presentation of the processed data to the system user. Clearly the format of the presentation will depend heavily on the application for which the system is designed. For example, there would be little point in presenting an air traffic controller with a lineprinter listing of the planes considered most likely to crash. Clearly such an application would require a highly interactive, real-time, user-friendly interface based upon a graphical display of some sort.

It can be seen, therefore, that the requirements placed upon the design of such a system by both the sampling and the presentation sub-systems can be equally demanding. The affect of their inclusion in any system design must be carefully tested and assessed, to ensure that the resulting system will not malfunction under extreme operational conditions such as a heavy loading.

Perhaps more typically, the Sample and Present sub-system interfaces may be handled manually. For instance, information about the real world may be sampled and translated into a suitable data format for submission to the processing sub-system by liveware - a computer operator. Manual submission of data via a keyboard is less restrictive on any timing constraints and is much easier to implement (this may be the only way of submitting data to a program running on a microcomputer). Likewise 'output' information may be presented to the user in textual format either on a monitor or on a printer. This is by far the most common type of interfacing mechanism and every attempt should bemade during the design stages to ensure a user-friendly interface.

Irrespective of whether the input and output mechanisms are manual or automatic the aim is still the same: to get information into and out of the processing sub-system components. In practice, the activities of the processing sub-system may well be functionally decomposed so as to be carried out by a number of separate modules. Within such an arrangement, each module of the processing sub-system operates in series with another, the input data being received by one module being that which was generated as output data by a previous module operating at this sub-functional

level; in like fashion, this module will produce output data for
subsequent consumption by its successor module. Figure 4.2 illustrates the
concept for the Sample sub-system.

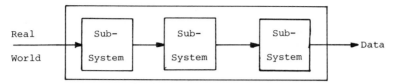

Fig 4.2 The Sample sub-system

Data analysis is concerned with identifying the requirements for data to
be input to a system, and output from it. At its most basic, this could
mean concentrating solely on input and output requirements - the
interface with the environment - for the system as a whole. However, given
the idea of a hierarchy of sub-systems, all parts of which have their own
input/output interfaces, data analysis can equally well be further
refined so as to cover sub-systems as well.

Moreover, the Processing Function also has its inputs and outputs; after
all, its role in life is effectively to transform in some way the former
into the latter. Carried out to its fullest, therefore, data analysis will
also embrace the Processing sub-systems and their input/output interfaces.

What is required, inevitably, is a notation in which the analysis can be
represented for consumption by all members of the design team.

4.2 Data Flow Analysis

There are a number of design notations in existence, all of which share
the common aim of being consistent and complete representations of a
software system.Since a comparative study of design notations is somewhat
beyond the scope of this book, we will be content with a description and
demonstration of one approach, Data Flow Diagrams, in terms of their value
during the various software development stages.

Data flow diagrams are used in the functional description of (sub-)systems
by showing how the input data of a processing component is transformed
to output data. In so doing, they describe how the data is generated and
used at each of the intermediate stages. Data flow diagrams were first
propose by Yourdon and Constantine (1979) and, although presented in
various forms in the literature, they typically consist of three components:

* Circles representing the functions performed at the intermediate
  stages.

* Arrowed lines with suitable annotations alongside highlighting what the data object is.

* The operators * and +.

The circles represent the tranformations performed on the data objects identified by the annotated arrow lines. Wherever possible one should adhere to the convention whereby all inputs to a process arrive from the left; all outputs from an intermediate process are generated on the right. Consequently the information flow through the entire group of sub-systems should be from left to right.

The * and + operators are used to describe the relationship between the data objects that either arrive, or are generated by a process. The * operator means that all the surrounding arrowed lines are required as inputs by this process, whereas the + operator means that only one of the surrounding data objects identified by the arrowed lines is required by the process. On output the * operator means that all of the data objects surrounding it are to be generated; the + operator means that only one of the surrounding objects will be generated.

Data flow diagrams only show how the output data is generated from the input data, they do not relect any control or sequencing information. During the description of a system's operation each process circle may be regarded as a black box which performs the suitable operation on the inputs to produce the respective outputs. A detailed description of its operation is not necessary.

Consider, as an example, the telephone directory system which was introduced in Chapter 3. This was required to offer three major functions, namely Addition, Modification and Search; we assume that each becomes a module in our system design. Two further modules, User Interface and Disc Output are specified in addition. Details of data flow for each of the five modules are as follows:

User Interface Module

Prompts the user for the next command which could be one of either:

* Add a new entry to the database.
* Modify an existing entry.
* Search for a particular telephone number or name.

The outputs to the user include: reporting error messages, and displaying retrieved information. The inputs received from the user depend upon the function selected, but would include: Name of entry, telephone number and the function to be performed. One of the functions of this module would be to decipher the received information and select the appropriate module for execution.The outputs generated depend upon the module selected for execution; for the 'Add a record' and 'Modify a record' modules both the name and telephone number are issued, whereas for the 'Search' module either the name or the telephone number are generated.

Add a Record

Receives both name and telephone number from the user interface module. It then proceeds to convert this information into a suitable format for storage on the disc. It would also generate a file pointer within its local tables for easy system access.

Modify a Record

Receives name and telephone number, and generates either an amended record details for storage on the disc, or an error to the user interface module.

<u>Search for a Record</u>

Searches for a name or a telephone number. It outputs to the user interface module either the details of the requested entry, or an error message.

<u>Output to Disc</u>

Receives information to be formatted for onward transmission to the disc drive.

The data flow diagram for this example is as shown in figure 4.3. It clearly shows what data is used by each of the identified modules.

4.3   Data Structures

Data may take various forms - it depends upon the information it is intended to represent. For instance, if a system needs to sample and represent temperature then there are two immediate questions that need to be answered. Firstly, is the temperature going to be on a Farenheit or Celsius scale? Secondly, to what accuracy does the temperature have to be held? Clearly any algorithm operating on such data has to be sure exactly what format the data is arriving in. The choice over what is the best format inevitably depends on the hardware options which are available - which means those provided by the manufacturer of the host computer.

Computer manufacturers have to make a trade-off in their designs between providing a high degree of accuracy - with associated high costs, and relatively low accuracy- with comparatively low costs. The choice depends upon the availability of such items as memory modules, arithmetic logic units, CPU, all of which need to be compatible in terms of the number of bits per memory location. In an attempt to standardise the situation most computer components are produced to either 8, 16, or 32 bits in 'length'. All data items have to be represented, ultimately, in a manner dictated by this processor bit-length.

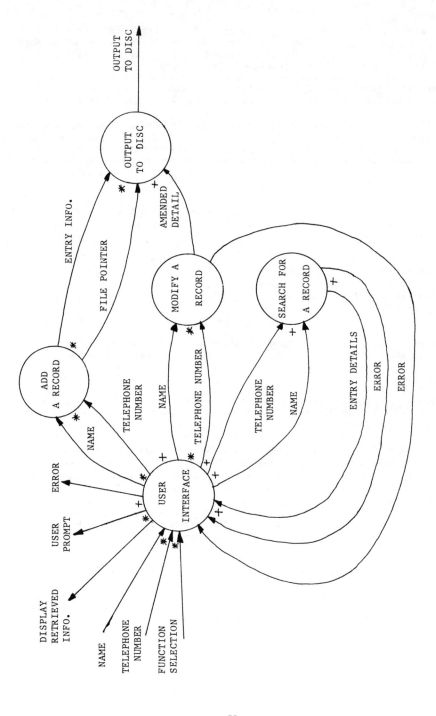

Fig. 4.3   Data Flow Diagram for Telephone Directory System

52

As regards the processor instruction set, three basic data handling capabilities are generally provided: for characters, integers and floating point numbers. Whatever programming notation - language - is employed, all information ultimately has to be coded, stored, processed and presented using these data formats. However, this is not to say that the software engineer has to be bound by these three data types. All but the most primitive programming languages build upon these basic types to provide data structuring facilities of their own, translating use of these features into the machine-level equivalents as part of their transalation role.

In this way, software design is aided by the design of the programming language which is to be used to implement that design. Although the choice of language is ideally left until design is complete (but see Chapter 7 on this point), an awareness of programming language capabilities is a practical necessity. Data analysis, and the choice of how that data is to be structured, will therefore be influenced by the data structuring features; data flow between the software and its environment, by the input/output features.

4.4 Data Handling in Basic and Pascal

The BBC microcomputer is widely used, and few students will not have met one in their travels. It has its own 'structured' version of BASIC - BBC BASIC. A small range of other programming languages are available for the machine, one of which is known as ISO Pascal - a version of Pascal which conforms to the International Standards Organisation standard for the the language

Throughout this book we shall be illustrating various points by means of examples in the programming languages BBC BASIC and ISO Pascal. Although not ideal choices (perhaps) as languages for software engineering, many students will learn BASIC - often through teaching themselves - as their first programming language, moving on to study Pascal as part of a formal programming or software engineering course. The reader is expected to have a working knowledge of both languages in what follows.

4.4.1 DATA DECLARATIONS AND SCOPE

Before moving on to data structures themselves, it is necessary to mention some of the data handling ground rules for both languages.

Each instance of a data object in a software system is given a 'variable name' by which it can be identified and referenced throughout the program to which it relates. In addition, variable names also have an important role during the testing and validation stages of the software system for they are used to identify the variables used in the integration of all the individual modules.

Clearly it is advantageous to choose unique, meaningful names wherever possible to enhance clarity and avoid ambiguity. Some languages impose severe restrictions on their naming conventions which do not always allow this to happen. Early versions of BASIC severely restricted the choice of variable names, although later versions, such as BBC BASIC, are much more flexible in this respect.

Every variable has to be declared. This will be done either explicitly or implicitly, depending on the language, with explicit declarations being much less prone to error. Associated with this declaration of the variable name will be a definition of its type - the units, if you like, of the value that the name represents.

Pascal requires all data objects to be explicitly identified before they are used, irrespective of whether they appear in a main program or a sub-program. The general form of a program layout is:

> Program header - Title and input/output information;
>
> Label declarations;
> Constant declarations;
> Type declarations;
> Variable declarations;
> Procedure/function declarations;
> . . . .
> Statement part.

This rigid structuring is carried through into the declaration of the sub-program elements, procedures and functions, each of which must follow a similar pattern:

> Procedure/function (parameter list);
>
> Label declarations;
> Constant declarations;
> Type declarations;
> Variable declarations;
> Procedure/function declarations;
> . . . .
> Statement part;

One of the major disadvantages of BASIC is that there is no declarative section where all the variables that are intended to be used are clearly identified. Variables are declared implicitly, as a result of their first appearance in an assignment statement, at any place within a module/ program. Also the type of variable being represented is defined by the variable name for which there is a pre-defined default option. The best that can be done to aid comprehension is to have a liberal distribution of suitable comments which clearly identify variable names with their type. In BBC BASIC procedures and functions are usually declared at the end of the of the main program, but again there is no mandatory structure imposed by the language.

Pascal, therefore, by virtue of the fact that it requires certain entities to be in a certain order, and declared prior to their use, almost enforces the software writer to adopt a structured approach. BASIC, on the other hand, with its absence of structure, virtually invites the programmer to write code in large, monolithic chunks.

The 'scope of a variable' is a term used to describe the areas of a program's structure within which that variable may be referenced (used). In Pascal, a variable which is declared in the main program is said to be global, i.e. may be referenced by any statement either in the main program or in any sub-program. A variable declared within a sub-program is said to be local to that sub-program and as such may only be referenced by a statement either in that sub-program or in a nested sub-program. A variable that is locally declared with a name that is the same as the one that is declared globally is regarded as a totally different variable. Figure 4.4 illustrates the different levels of scope.

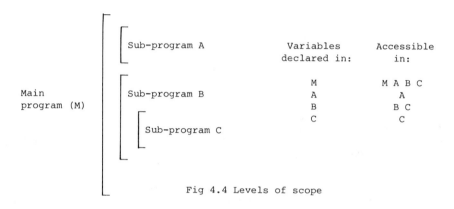

Fig 4.4 Levels of scope

In BBC BASIC, all variables are considered to be global apart from those declared locally within sub-programs. Local variables are exactly the same as globals, except that they are declared in a sub-program prefixed by the reserved word LOCAL. This special word tells the BASIC interpreter that the following identifiers are for reference by this sub-program only.

Identifying the scope of a variable is particularly important when using a design tool such as data flow diagrams, for it is the identification of the data objects - and the operations performed upon them - that is important to the designer. The adoption of such a structured approach as having a series of modules with clearly identifiable data objects is of considerable assistance to the design process as a whole.

Data objects that are global pose a problem for they are clearly accessible by all executable statements and, as such, do not actually flow. Life would be much simpler if the use of globally declared data objects were outlawed, since the referencing of every data object would then be much easier to detect. In situations where it is not possible to outlaw their use care must be exerted to ensure that all data objects referenced by a module are adequately documented. This is particularly important during development when there may well be many refinements to the design which must be documented to ensure consistency.

4.4.2 REALS, INTEGERS AND CHARACTERS

We look firstly at the data structures which reflect the architectural aspects of the underlying hardware: real, integer and character values. In both BASIC and Pascal, we assume that the method of representation is the same, e.g.

* Real held in mantissa/exponent form, using 5 x 8-bit bytes

* Integer held as 4 x 8-bit bytes

* Characters (in ASCII code) held either singly in one 8-bit byte, or in 'string' form in a sequence of consecutive bytes

4.4.2.1 Real variables

In BASIC any variable name will be taken, by default, to represent a real value. Real variables have a greater range than integers and can be used to represent real world entities. For example most of the standard mathematical formulae would be almost useless if constant whole numbers were used to represent such numerical phenomena as 'pi'. Similarly the use of the computer in determining the results of mathematical equations would be severely restricted if only integer division was available. Real variables can be used to store numbers in the range:

$$2 \times 10^{38} \quad \text{to} \quad -2 \times 10^{39}$$

although they are only stored to a 9 digit accuracy on the BBC microcomputer. Real numbers may be specified either in real form

e.g.   20   My_weight = 198.56

or in Exponent-form

e.g.   20   My_weight = 1.9856E2   or
        20   My_weight = 19856.0E-2

where E can be translated to mean 'times ten to the power of ...'. Variables introduced in this way are easy to identify as real variables for they have a decimal point in their definition. Real variables that are assigned real numbers that do not have a decimal point are not so easy to identify by a person not conversant with BASIC.

In Pascal all variables have to be declared prior to their use in an executable statement. As in BASIC their numeric value may be specified in either a real form or an E-form. The declaration appears in the VARiable declaration section of the program module, i.e. either the main program or a procedure/function.

e.g.

|

```
VAR
        My_Weight : REAL;
        MyWifesWeight : REAL;
        MySonsWeight : REAL;
```

|

```
BEGIN
```

|

```
        My_Weight := 198.56;
        MyWifesWeight := 29768.0E-2;
        MySonsWeight := 0.7349E2;
```

|

```
END.
```

The number range of these variables is identical to those available in BASIC.

4.4.2.2 Integer variables.

In BASIC an integer variable is specified by terminating the variable name with the special character '%'. Integers are whole numbers which, on the BBC microcomputer, are held accurately to 1-digit within the range:

$$-2\ 147\ 483\ 648 \quad to \quad 2\ 147\ 483\ 647$$

Integer variables are used to define exact entities such as the number of times a statement has been executed, or the number of members in a family. (Although the national average, it is actually unusual to have 2.347 people in a family.) Integer numbers are specified as expected:

e.g.   30   My_age_is% = 21

In Pascal an integer variable identifier is identical to that of a real variable identifier. Integer variables are also declared within the VAR declaration section.

e.g.

|

```
        VAR
```

```
                My_Age : INTEGER;
                MyWifesAge : INTEGER;
                MySonsAge : INTEGER;


                        |


        BEGIN


                        |


                My_Age := 21;
                MyWifesAge := 29;
                MySonsAge := 4;


                        |


        END.
```

The range for an integer variable is identical to that available in BASIC
on the BBC microcomputer.

4.4.2.3 Characters

Individual characters can be manipulated in BASIC, but are more commonly
grouped together to form 'strings', represented by 'string variables'.
Such variables are denoted by the special terminating character '$'.
Assignments to a string variable would typically look like

        e.g.   40   Name$ = "Frank Smith"

In BBC BASIC, the maximum number of characters which can be assigned to a
string variable is 255 (the maximum value of an 8-bit integer - which is
the way in which the string length is held). String variables provide the
programmer with an easy mechanism for manipulating characters which, when
used effectively, can give the program's input and output an attractive,
aesthetic quality which is essential for a user-friendly program.

In Pascal character variables have to declared in the VARiable section as
with all other variables. No special indication is needed regarding the
format of the identifier. Character variables can only be used to hold a
single character; character strings have to use a rather unsatisfactory
mechanism known as a 'packed array' which effectively defines the string
as a series of individual characters:

        e.g.
```
                        |

        VAR
                        |


                Letter : CHAR;
                Operator : CHAR;
                NameOfClient : PACKED ARRAY [1..11] OF CHAR;


                        |
```

58

```
        BEGIN
                        |

                Letter := 'q';
                Operator := '*';
                NameOfClient := 'Frank Smith';


                        |

        END.
```

4.4.2.4 Limitations

Whilst real, integer and character variables may represent the hard data
of any computing application, basing data analysis and design solely on
these three entities would be very unsatisfactory - rather like designing
a house purely in terms of bricks and panes of glass. So, in much the same
way that house analysis is actually carried out in terms of rooms,
double-glazing and fitted wardrobes, so a high-level programming language
will aid data analysis by providing a number of 'internal' data structures
for the designer to use.

In the following sections we consider some of these structures, and their
role in life.

4.4.3 CONSTANTS

Constants are data objects which do not vary during the execution of a
program. Such objects may be either numeric (i.e. real or integer), a
single character or a character string. In Pascal constants are declared
using the reserved word CONST, followed by a list of constant identifiers
and their associated values, each separated by a semi-colon:

```
e.g.            CONST
                        Page_length = 60 ;
                        Pi = 3.1415927 ;
                        Space = ' ' ;
                        Add_operator = '+' ;
```

The scope of a constant may be either local or global, depending where it
is declared.

Now, on the face of it, a constant may not seem to be much of a structure.
As with an iceberg, however, most of what matters lies under the surface.
If a variable is declared as a constant then its value cannot be altered
by an assignment statement during program execution, any attempt to do so
being flagged as an error. This is rather nice from a software engineering
viewpoint since it eliminates the possiblity of it being altered anywhere
else in the program.

During data analysis, therefore, identification of constant values should

always be undertaken thoroughly since the benefits will be reaped throughout the project development.

BASIC does not have any mechanism by which constants may be distinguished
from variables. Consequently there is no assurance that the constant value
remains unaltered - since a variable may appear on the left hand side of
any assignment statement. Whether such an action is deliberate or
accidental is irrelevant; its potential as a source of error should be
sufficient give a software engineer nightmares.

4.4.4 BOOLEAN

Certain types of information are not of a numeric or character form - for
example, notification of whether a database has been updated since it was
last archived is simply a yes/no reply. Of course this could be implemented by using a real or integer variable which takes the value of, say,
3 to stand for yes and 5 for no. However, not only is this artificial, but
it means that fault diagnosis requires the software engineer to continually translate between values. Boolean variables are designed to be used
with this yes/no, on/off, true/false sort of information.

Boolean variables in BASIC are represented by any identifier - it is the
manner of its use that determines the fact that it is a boolean. However,
since a 'false' condition is actually held, and printed, as a 0 (zero),
and 'true' as -1 (although any non-zero value is actually taken to be
true), it is common to use an integer variable as a boolean.

                30   Is_it_raining% = TRUE
     e.g.   35   State% = X > Y

The major diifficulty in using Boolean variables in BASIC is that of
distinguishing between them and real/integer variables. Unless there is
very good accompanying documentation confusion can be rife.

In Pascal Boolean variables have to be declared in the variable declaration section with suitable identifiers being selected. The format of
these identifiers is the same as for all other variables. The 'false'
condition is actually implemented using the value of zero, whilst 'true'
has the value of one.

     e.g.

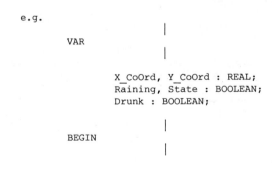

          VAR

                   X_CoOrd, Y_CoOrd : REAL;
                   Raining, State : BOOLEAN;
                   Drunk : BOOLEAN;

          BEGIN

```
                    Raining := TRUE;
                    WetWeekend := Raining OR Drunk;
                    State := X_CoOrd > Y_CoOrd;

                          |

          END.
```

4.4.5 TYPES

The binary condition represented by a boolean variable is one particular
example from the real world of a data object which cannot easily be represented in BASIC. There are many others. For example, consider the design
of a database which will be used by a company to maintain a list of its
current stock. Amongst the stock items might be:

          cycle, ball, car, book, doll, bat

In BASIC these might each be represented by an integer v_riable, ITEM%,
which would be allocated a value depending upon the particular object
being represented, e.g. ITEM% = 0 for a cycle, ITEM% = 1 for a ball, ITEM%
= 2 for a car, etc. Such a representation requires continual translation
between the integer values of 0, 1, 2, etc., and the object being
represented. Expert knowledge of the program structure, the translation
between data objects and their representative values, together with an
understanding of how the objects are being manipulated is essential if the
program is to be maintained once in service.

Pascal provides an answer to this problem by allowing the declaration of
the software engineer's own data types, and variables associated with that
type:

          e.g.
                          |

              TYPE
                          |

                    Object = (Cycle, Ball, Car, Book, Doll, Bat);

                          |

              VAR
                          |

                    Item : Object;
                    Part : Object;

                          |

In a program segment these 'type' variables may be used much as ordinary
variables, except that they cannot be used in arithmetic expressions.

```
e.g.    BEGIN

                        |

                 Part := Cycle;
                 Item := Part;
                 Part := Doll;

                        |

        END.
```

Clearly the identification of the data objects in such an explicit manner maximises visibility and fully enables the designer to adequately assess how the individual items are being manipulated. Indoing so the designer is able to get a better understanding of the overall effect of what the program is trying to do. Such visibilty enables maintenance of the program to be taken on more readily by another programmer at a later date. Benefits from such visibilty are found in all aspects of the software life cycle, from design where design reviews (see Chapter 6) are easier, to testing where an in-depth understanding of all system components and their interactions is essential.

The effect on data analysis and design is to provide freedom. Requirements for input and output data can be considered in real-world terms, without a major question mark of 'can this be implemented' hanging over every part of the exercise. The fact that the final implementation then bears a very strong resemblance in data representation to the specified requirements is no bad thing either.

4.4.6 SUBRANGES

The identification during data analysis of a particular item of data, and its type, is reflected, as we have seen, in the data declaration. A full analysis will go further and identify the allowable range of values for each data item in order that validation checks can be conducted.

Pascal facilitates this by means of its subrange option to a data declaration, allowing the software writer to specify upper and lower data values for integer, character and user defined types. Thus, instead of a simple VAR declaration like

        VAR   My_age : INTEGER;

which effectively says that variable My_age can assume any value in the default range (-2147483648 to 2147483647!), we would use a more realistic subrange declaration such as

        VAR   My_age : 1 .. 100; {Software engineers aren't
                           expected to live for more than 100 years}

A general form of a subrange is

                    < lower bound > .. < upper bound >

with the above example stating that the subrange for variable My_age is
the set of integer values between between 1 and 100. In this way the range
of values that a variable can take on are restricted: My_age cannot exceed
100, and a negative value is impossible! If we wanted to take into consideration the possibility of a lifespan increasing through future wonders of
medical science, the declaration could be modified to become

            VAR   My_age : 1 .. MAXINT;

where MAXINT is a shorthand way of specifying the machine's maximum
positive integer. In fact the default declaration of INTEGER is equivalent
to -MAXINT .. MAXINT. This notation is very useful since it not only says
explicitly the data values that may be taken on by a variable, but also
remove the confusion and necessity of knowing exactly the ranges of a
particular machine.

In the case of REALs data values are always in accordance with the default
settings for there is no way that the upper and lower data values for a
REAL variable may be specified, due to the inherent accuracy with which
the numbers are held. The default setting for character variables, CHAR,
is normally the character set of the machine in terms of ASCII or EBCDIC
codes.

Subrange values may also be specified with user-defined types,

        e.g.   CONST
                        Age_limit = 100;
                        Sample_space = 5;
                TYPE
                        Letter : 'a' .. 'z';
                        Digit : '0' .. '9';
              . VAR
                        My_age : 1 .. Age_limit;
                        Alpha : Letter;
                        Beta : Digit;
                        Sample : -Sample_space .. Sample_space;

                BEGIN
                                    |

                        Alpha := 'd';   { Is O.K.   }
                        Beta := '8';   { Is also O.K. }
                        Sample := 4;   { So is this! }

                                    |
                END.

Subrange declarations provide information of expected data values, meaning
that the results of data analysis are again carried through into the final
software design. Because BASIC provides no such mechanism, a gap between
the results of analysis, design and programming is unavoidably created
with documentation having to perform the bridging function once more.

4.4.7 ARRAYS

On many occasions data analysis will indicate that a grouping of similar data objects is required. A number of structures are provided to assist in the manipulation of such groups, the most basic of which is the array. Access to a particular object in an array is achieved using the array name and the offset within that array. In BASIC all entries in a given array have to be of the same type - real, integer, string or boolean variables - mixtures not being permitted.

Before use, the format of the array has to be stated, (one- or two-dimensional) together with the maximum number of entries in each dimension. This is achieved through the use of a DIM statement, which at least clearly identifies the data structure and its characteristics in one single statement. A software engineer's dream. Access to a single data object can be effected through the array's index (or subscript, as it is more commonly known).

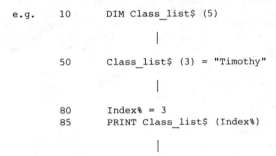

```
      e.g.   10      DIM Class_list$ (5)


             50      Class_list$ (3) = "Timothy"


             80      Index% = 3
             85      PRINT Class_list$ (Index%)
```

In the above example Class_list$ is an array of 6 locations, each capable of storing a string variable. The locations are identified by Class_list$ (0), Class_list$ (1), through to Class_list$ (5).

Arrays in BASIC may have up to two dimensions. In the above example a second dimension may be easily added to hold, say, the corresponding address of each class member entry since that, too, would be a string variable. However. if there was a requirement to hold an integer value in this second dimension - an attendance figure or record of marks, for instance - then this would have to be held within a second array. Any association between entries in separate arrays is achieved through the index

```
      e.g.   10      DIM Class_list$ (5) , Attendance% (5)


             80      Index% = 3
             85      PRINT Class_list$ (Index%), Attendance% (Index%)
```

64

There can be a problem with the imposed restriction that the array index always starts at 0 and goes up to the maximum declared, for this may not represent the real-world situation. For example if the array is to hold values of some variable X, say, for temperatures ranging from -25 to +25 degrees Centigrade, then this would require the declaration of an array of 51 locations:

```
10        DIM Array (50)
```

Each location would be identified by an index value in the range of 0 to 50. Consequently there would need to be continual translation between -25 to 25, and 0 to 50, with increased scope for error.

In Pascal the array declaration specifies not only the size of the array and the type of data object being represented, but also the upper and lower bounds of its dimensions. The declaration of an array in Pascal to hold the data values in the range of -25 to 25, as described above, would be:

```
VAR      Sample_space : ARRAY [-25 .. 25] OF INTEGER;
```

Access to array elements uses the standard indexing procedure, where the index variable would have an associated subrange:

```
e.g.    VAR
                Sample_space : ARRAY [-25 .. 25] OF INTEGER;
                Index : -25 .. 25;
        BEGIN
                        |
                Index := 4;
                Sample_space [Index] := Sample_space [Index] + 1 ;

                        |
        END.
```

There are no restrictions on the of number of dimensions an array can have in Pascal, unlike BASIC where the upper limit is two dimensions. Although this may seem an attractive feature at first, it can lead to intolerable confusion when the number of dimensions become excessive. In addition, it is difficult to see how any real-world data analysis could prompt the use of a data structure having more than three dimensions!

There is no mechanism for the declaration of variable length arrays in Pascal, i.e. there is no facility for declarations like

```
VAR      Size : ARRAY [1 .. N] OF REAL;
```

where N is supplied at run-time. This is seen to be rather limiting by some, although such flexibility can often lead to confusion, particularly during the testing phase.

Pushing the idea of visibility - the clarity of the relationships between analysis, design and program - somewhat further, it should be pointed out

65

that any set of real-world objects might need to be processed by use of an array-like structure. In Pascal it is possible to have arrays of integer, real, boolean, character or any user defined type. There is no equivalent of the string variable that are available in BASIC, although Pascal does have PACKED ARRAYs which can be used to store strings of characters.

For instance if it is necessary to maintain a record of all the items held within a toy shop, with the assumption that there is to be no more than 100 of each item, then the program declarations would look something like:

```
    TYPE
        Object : ( Cycle, Ball, Car, Book, Doll, Bat );
        Object_limit : 1 .. 100;
        Stock_control : ARRAY [Object] of Object_limit;

    VAR
        ShopA_Stock_Level : Stock_control ;
        ShopB_Stock_Level : Stock_control ;

                            |

    BEGIN

                            |

        ShopA_Stock_Level [Cycle] := ShopA_Stock_Control [Cycle] + 1;
        ShopB_Stock_Level [Bat] := ShopB_Control_Level [Bat] + 1;

                            |

    END.
```

An equivalent program written in BASIC would be instantly unrecognisable, requiring continual conversion between the objects and their internal representation as either integers or characters. It is left as an exercise for the reader to write a BASIC counterpart with which to compare the above. Don't spend too many weeks on it: just long enough to appreciate how visible the object representation and its manipulation actually is in the Pascal version.

Program modification is made that much easier through using meaningful data structures. Consider an extension to the shop application in which it is now required to record, on a day-by-day basis, all the objects which are sold in each of a number of shops over a period of 5 weeks:

```
    CONST
        Stock_limit = 100;
        Max_week_No = 5;

    TYPE
        Object : (Cycle, Ball, Car, Book, Doll, Bat);
        Day : (Monday, Tuesday, Wednesday, Thursday, Friday, Saturday);
        Shop_list : ( ShopA, ShopB, ShopC, ShopD, ShopE, ShopF );

    VAR
        Company_record : ARRAY [Shop_list,Day,Object, 1 .. Max_Week_No]
                                        OF 1 .. Stock_limit ;
```

```
BEGIN

                                    |

        Company_record [ ShopF, Friday, Bat, 3 ] := 5 ; {This means
            that ShopF sold 5 Bats on Friday of week number 3}

        Company_record [ ShopA, Monday, Cycle, 1 ] := 7 ; {Similarly,
            this means that ShopA sold 7 Cycles on Monday of week 1}

                                    |

    END.
```

To say that a similar program sequence in BASIC would be both complex and
totally confusing to the uninitiated is probably an understatement.

4.4.8 RECORDS

There are some applications where data objects are not single data items
and, unlike array elements, not all of the same type. For example, a data
object representing personnel information may contain the following items
and types:

Name	–	Character
Address	–	Character
Age	–	Integer
Sex	–	Male, female
Marital status	–	Single, married
Number of children	–	Integer
Salary	–	Integer

Needless to say, there is no mechanism in BASIC for the explicit representation of such a data structure. In Pascal, however, information such as
this may be represented within a single data structure, called a RECORD.
The declaration would be along the following lines:

```
    CONST
        Character_length = 10;

    TYPE
        Age_limit = 1 .. 100;
        String_length : 1 .. Character_length;
        String : PACKED ARRAY [ String_length ] OF CHAR;
        Personnel_details =

    RECORD
        Name : String; {string of 10 characters }
        Address : ARRAY [ 1 .. 4 ] OF String; { The address is
                considered to be 4 lines of 10 characters }
        Age : Age_limit;
        Sex : ( Male, Female );
        Marital_status : ( Single, Married );
        Number_of_children : 1 .. 20: { Perhaps a bit excessive }
```

```
        Salary : 1 .. 30000; { Just being optimistic }
    END; { That completes the definition of the Personnel_details
        RECORD structure }

VAR
    Maggies_details : Personnel_details;

BEGIN
                        |

    Maggies_details.Name := 'M J Smythe'; { 10 characters
                                    including spaces }
    Maggies_details.Address [ 1 ] := '2 Dummy St';
    Maggies_details.Address [ 2 ] := 'Somewhere ';
    Maggies_details.Address [ 3 ] := 'Nuttshire ';
    Maggies_details.Address [ 4 ] := ' NOTT 1IN ';
    Maggies_details.Age := 23;
    Magiies_details.Sex := Female;
    Maggies_details.Marital_status := Single;
    Maggies_details.Number_of_children := 0;
    Maggies_details.Salary := 9563;

                        |

END.
```

The information being represented is visible as are the manipulations being performed on it. The rather cumbersome way of referencing an individual attribute of a record variable

< record variable name > . < attribute name >

can be replaced by the equally clear WITH statement; for instance, the statements of the above example are completely equivalent to:

```
        WITH Maggies_details DO
        BEGIN
            Name := 'M J Smythe'; { 10 characters including spaces }
            Address [ 1 ] := '2 Dummy St';
            Address [ 2 ] := 'Somewhere ';
            Address [ 3 ] := 'Nuttshire ';
            Address [ 4 ] := ' NOTT 1IN ';
            Age := 23;
            Sex := Female;
            Marital_status := Single;
            Number_of_children := 0;
            Salary := 9563;
        END; { Marks end of the WITH statement }
```

The above examples clearly demonstrate the visibility offered by using such a data structure. Efficiency may also be gained through the use of VARIANT RECORDS. These are similar in format to the RECORD structure presented above except that it incorporates slectivity, i.e. only those parts of the data structure that are to be used during this execution will be allocated. In the above example there is no point in having an

attribute for Number_of_children if the Marital_status is single -
assuming a morally perfect society of course. The advantages of VARIANT
RECORDS are in the savings in storage. However they do introduce a level
of complexity and uncertainty during testing and evaluation phases.

Finally, it is possible to have an array of RECORDs. For instance, an extensions to the above example might be to formulate a Personnel_file data
structure from the collection of Personnel_details:

```
        CONST
            Number_of_employees = 50;

        TYPE
            Personnel_file : ARRAY [ 1 .. Number_of_employees ] OF
                                                Personnel_details;
        VAR
            FactoryA_file : Personnel_file;

        BEGIN
                        |
            WITH FactoryA_file [ 33 ] DO  { Assume entry for employee
                                number 33 is being manipulated }
            BEGIN
                        |

                Name := 'P K Keeper';
                Age := 56;


                        |

            END;
                        |

        END.
```


4.4.9 POINTERS

Arrays and Records are sturctures which contain a number of data items in
a defined sequence: array alement 1 is followed in the structure by array
element 2, and so on. In this way, processing of the data structure will
also proceed sequentially. However, data analysis may well conclude that a
requirement exists for a structure which is not organised in this way;
that has the capability, for instance, of being searched in a non-
sequential manner, or of being dynamically expanded and contracted during
program execution. What we are talking about here is a list structure, in
which the data elements are accompanied by additional 'pointer'
information serving to link them to other elements in the same structure.
In some ways we might consider this an ultimate test of the data
structuring capability offered by a language.

BASIC would fail the test miserably. A linked structure would have to be
based on the highest level data structure available, the array, with one
dimension of the array holding data elements and another holding the index
value of the item to which that entry was linked - as shown in figure 4.5.

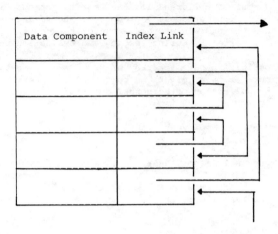

Data Component	Index Link

Fig. 4.5 Implementation of a linked structure in BASIC

In addition it would be neccesary to declare an array of sufficient size to accommodate the largest list possible. Needless to say, being able to track ones way through such a maze would require expert knowledge of the intricacies of the interconnection mechanism.

In Pascal POINTER variables, together with the built-in procedures called NEW and DISPOSE, are available. POINTER variables are declared in the TYPE declaration section prior to the RECORD structure at which they are going to point. A typical application of POINTER variables is in the construction of a simple linked list, as shown in figure 4.6.

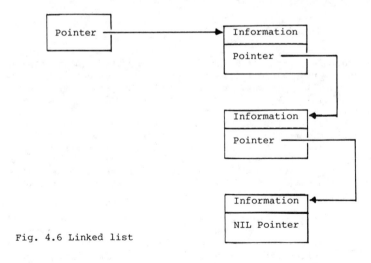

Fig. 4.6 Linked list

For instance, instead of constructing a Personnel_file as an array of

Personnel_details it would be possible to construct a Personnel_file as a linked-list in the form shown above. To do this it is necessary to define a POINTER which will point to the beginning of the list, and to include a POINTER within the RECORD structure itself to accommodate the internal linkage mechanism between the individual records. The declaration of such a structure would be:

```
            TYPE
                        |

                Link = ^Personnel_details;
                Personnel_details =

            RECORD
                        |

                Salary : 1 .. 30000;
                Next_entry : Link;
            END; { of updated Personnel_details RECORD structure }

            VAR
                        |

                Personnel_file : Link; { definition of initial POINTER
                        variable which will point to the first entry in
                        the linked list }
                Component : Link; { general POINTER variable used in the
                        creation and manipulation of the linked-list }
                Tail : Link; { points to the last entry in the list }

                        |
```

The character '^' is used to denote that the variable is to be treated as a POINTER variable which will be associated with the dynamic storage of the associated RECORD structure. A POINTER variable is the only way of referencing dynamic storage. The initial value of a POINTER is NIL - this represents an unassigned variable. The general sequence of events is:

* Create a new component of the type identified by the POINTER variable using the built-in procedure called NEW;

* Attach the newly created component to the existing structure.

* If it is the first component then it is simply assigned to the POINTER variable which points to the first entry in the queue.

* If the component is no longer required then the allocated storage can be released, for subsequent allocation to another newly created component.

71

Construction of a Personnel_file linked list would then be achieved in the following manner:

```
    BEGIN
            |
        NEW ( Component ); { create the first entry }
        Personnel_file := Component ; { assign it to the linked
            |                                     list POINTER }
        {assign values to its attributes}
        NEW ( Component ); { create next entry in the list }


            |  -

        WITH Component^ DO
        BEGIN
            |
           Age := 34; { assign values to the various attributes of
                   the RECORD structure }
            |
           Next := NIL; { NIL is used to indicate end of list }
            |
        END; { of WITH statement }

        Personnel_file^.Next := Component; { attach component to list }
        Tail := Component; { indicate end of the list }
            |
        NEW ( Component ); { create new component }
            |
        { assign values to its attributes }
            |
        Tail^.Next := Component ; { attach newly created component to
                                     end of the list }
        Tail := Component; { restore the end of the list POINTER for
                                     next attachment }
            |
        DISPOSE ( Component ); { return component storage to free-space
                   for re-allocation }
            |
    END.
```

Using the POINTER variables in this way makes efficient use of available storage, whilst maximising on the visibility offered by Pascal. Although it may appear somewhat complex it isn't; in fact once one comes to grips with this type of dynamic storage mechanism it is easy to find your way around a program.

4.4.10 DATA FILES

The amount of data that needs to be handled largely dictates the mode of organisation. In the simplest case a requirement to sort 2 data objects into ascending order will need nothing more than 2 variables. If the number of data objects to be sorted is increased to 30 then it is a lot easier to use an array for this purpose. If the number increases such that they can no longer be held within the available memory then they have to be held within a data file.

BASIC provides some easy to use data file handling mechanisms for:

* opening a file
* closing a file
* obtaining a data object
* storing a data object
* obtaining a character
* storing a character
* checking for the end of the file

Data files provide a storage mechanism which is much more long term; the information can be used over much longer periods of time and is much more convenient for applications such as database management. In BBC BASIC data files are 'opened' by one of the following instructions as appropriate:

```
f% = OPENIN ("<filename>")  - for input files
f% = OPENOUT ("<filename>")  - for output files
f% = OPENUP ("<filename>")  - for files to be used for both input
                                                          and output
```

The type of data held within a file can be mixed in any way at all - but the arrangement obviously needs to be known by the author of any program which has to use the file. From the 'open' command onwards, all file input and output instructions would be defined in terms of a channel number, the file name no longer being used. This can lead to some confusion during fault finding since channel numbers convey no information as such, possibly only being related to the data analysis and design by accompanying documentation.

Pascal, on the other hand, requires all externally referenced files to be declared in the same way as variables:

```
e.g.    VAR
                    Data_file : FILE OF REAL;
                    Personnel_file : FILE OF CHAR;
                    Directory : TEXT; { same as FILE OF CHAR }
```

Their definition is clear and explicit, with any file reference also being clearly identified through the input/output statement. Externally referenced files are specified in the program header. For instance,

PROGRAM Telephone_directory (Input, Output, Personnel_file, Directory);

specifies Input and Output as the default input and output channels (the user terminal, normally) and Personnel_file and Directory are user defined files. The actual files used during a program run are specified via operating system commands prior to execution. Consequently, by simply altering the operating system commands, the same program may be used with any number of different actual files without altering the program itself. If the contents of a file alter then this can easily be accommodated through alteration of the file declaration section.

In addition to the basic input/output facilities there are a number of additional commands which are provided to assist in file manipulation:

    REWRITE (file_name) - initialises the file before writing to it,
                             from the beginning of the file.
    RESET (file_name)   - resets the file pointer to the beginning of
                             the file before reading any data from it.
    EOF (file_name)   - a boolean function which returns the value
                             TRUE if end of the file has been reached,
                             FALSE otherwise.

It is clearly evident that whatever the function being performed on data files in Pascal, the actual operation is explicitly defined. Again this makes the life of the software engineer that much easier.

4.5   Input and Output in Basic and Pascal

Having spent some time in looking at the data structures available within languages like BASIC and Pascal and their implications for data analysis, we return to the subject with which this chapter opened: input and output - the business of analysing the user's view of how data is to be supplied to the software, and results received from it. Again we will use BBC BASIC and ISO Pascal as the bases of our discussion.

In BASIC, the literature will suggest that there are two statements that can be used to get data into a program - INPUT or READ. We would argue that since READ only accesses data values that are embedded within the program already, it is not a true input statement at all but a facility for initialising variables. Consequently discussion of READ is deferred until Chapter 7.

The INPUT statement expects its data values to be supplied from either the keyboard or a data file - the keyboard is the default option if a file name is not specified. Irrespective of the source, the type of data supplied will be expected to be of the same type as that of the variable into it is to be stored. If the variable is of type integer then an integer value will be expected, and if a character or real value is supplied then an error will be generated.

Data can be read from a file by using an instruction of the form

        INPUT £ <channel number>, <list of variable names>

<channel number> having been previously set by an 'open' statement earlier in the program (see 4.4.10 above). Where the program is designed to be used interactively it is advisable to prompt the user for some data with a meaningful statement. This can either be achieved by outputting the relevant text using a PRINT statement or by incorporating the text within the INPUT instruction itself,

```
          INPUT " meaningful text " , variable name
```

Any aethestic text is acceptable, e.g.

```
     30  INPUT " X Co-ord = ", X_coord
     40  INPUT " Y Co-ord = ", Y_coord
```

|

```
     60  INPUT " Please supply surname for entry in directory - ", Name$
     70  INPUT " What is the street address ? ", Address$ (1)
     80  INPUT " And the town ? ", Address$ (2)
     90  INPUT " Postcode ? ", Address$ (3)
```

|

The incorporation of such user-friendly aspects as this should be standard practice; not every user will know what type of data to supply unless they are familiar with the program. Any software package that simply supplies a prompt like '?' should be burnt along with its writer.

An important part of data analysis, then, should be to determine not only what data is to be input from file and what from an interactive device, but also the form and the wording of the prompt messages.

The output generated by a program can either be displayed on the default device, usually a monitor or television screen, or be directed to a data file. All output generated by a BASIC program is achieved using the PRINT statement; its format is similar to the INPUT statement. Output to a data file is achieved using the instruction

```
          PRINT £ <channel number>, <variable name(s) or text>
```

The PRINT statement may be used either to output the contents of a variable, or just straight text enclosed between quotes. Where a display device is being used for output, the output format depends upon the punctuation of the PRINT statement itself: for instance, the symbol ',' means that the print values will be output on a field basis (i.e. integers and reals occupy so many character positions); a ';' between two variables suppresses any redundant spaces on output and at the end of a line suppresses the newline generation so that the next PRINT statement will follow on the same line - the rules rool, OK?

   e.g.

|

```
     250 PRINT "The name "; Name$; " is in the telephone directory "
     260 PRINT "and the address is ", Address$ (1)
```

|

would produce as output (if FRED had been input to Name$):

        The name FRED is in the telephone directory
        and the address is . . . .

The dependence upon special characters for establishing a printing format
means that the software engineer needs to know all the effects of their
use. Because it is not immediately obvious by looking at a program statement what the effect will be, the visibility between data analysis and the
final software is again diminished.

With Pascal, whatever input medium is employed, the input of data to the
program is via the statements READ or READLN. The format of the READ
statement is

        READ (<file name>, <variable name>);

The file name is optional, and if omitted, will result in the default
device being chosen, i.e. the keyboard. The type of data being supplied
must coincide with the type of the variable into which it is to be placed.
Any file name that is specified must be previously declared in the VAR
declaration section at the beginning of the program, e.g.

    VAR
                |

        My_record : Personnel_details;
        Directory : TEXT; { same as FILE OF CHAR }

                |

    BEGIN
                |

        READ (Directory, My_record.Name);   {read next 10 characters
                        from the file called Directory and place them into
                        the attribute Name of My_record}

                |

    END.

READLN can also be used to input data in the same way as READ, the only
difference being that anything remaining on that line after the values
have been read in are ignored. This is a potential area of concern to the
software engineer since it could lead to 'loss of data' during program
execution. The answer will lie in sound data analysis and data design,
grouping data items carefully and controlling their input through
meaningful prompt messages and rigorous validation.

Output generated by a Pascal program may be directed to either a data file
or display screen by means of a WRITE statement of the general form:

        WRITE (<file name>, <variable name>);

If the file name is omitted the default device is chosen, otherwise the
file name must appear in the VAR declaration section. Any text which is to

be printed should be enclosed between single quotes ('), e.g.

```
BEGIN                        |

    WRITE ('The name of the directory entry is', My_record.Name);
              {output the name of the directory entry to the
               default device, with supportive text}

                             |

END.
```

WRITELN has a similar effect to WRITE except that a newline character is issued after the values have been printed. Extensive use of WRITELN is likely to be necessary in order to meet well-analysed requirements for interactive presentation of output information.

As a final comparison the following statements are equivalent:

Activity	BASIC	Pascal
Suppress a newline	PRINT Data_value;	WRITE (Data_value);
Issue a newline	PRINT data_value	WRITELN (Data_value);
Print a blank line	PRINT	WRITELN;

From such a table it is evident that the functions being performed by each of these statements is more explicitly defined in Pascal than BASIC. It is also worth remembering that the file used during input/output operations are much more clearly identifiable in Pascal than the channel numbers that are used in BASIC.

4.6   Data Documentation

Documentation for data analysis is no less important than that for any other phase of the software life-cycle. Obviously the form that the documentation takes will depend on the analysis technique employed. By looking briefly at the associated documentation for use with data-flow diagrams, some general guidelines should become apparent.

When using data flow diagrams it is necessary to produce a checklist which associates every data object in a system with the modules that operate on it. Such information enables any subsequent design and/or development faults to be traced through the system, whilst simultaneously monitoring their effects. This information can either be gathered on a system wide basis, or on a module basis. The term 'Data Dictionary' is most commonly used to describe this type of documentation.

Basically a data dictionary contains a list of all the data objects in the system with, for each entry, associated information concerning such things as what the data object is representing in the real world, and the names of all modules which operate on that object.

Figure 4.7 below illustrates a typical entry in a paper-based data dictionary. The intention here, through a simple data documentation method, is to document for future reference the basic attributes of a module's data elements.

MODULE NAME =					
Data identifier	Input/ Output	Description	Associated modules	Units	Type

Fig. 4.7 A paper-based data dictionary

By creating such a dictionary from the beginnings of data analysis, and developing it through data design and program implementation, a complete documentary record can be established for subsequent use.

4.7 Summary

*   A computer system is a collection of functional sub-systems operating on well defined items of information.

*   Data flow diagrams show how the input data of a processing component is transformed into output data; in so doing, they portray the functional characteristics of the system and individual sub-systems.

*   Knowledge of the types of data structures provided by the computer system hardware is essential for the representation of real-world information.

*   Knowledge of higher-level data structures provided by a programming language is also essential, the comparative assessment of alternative data structures being a necessary part of software development.

*   User-defined data types provide many advantages and may well dictate the choice of implementation language.

*   The ease with which data can be obtained from, and presented to, either the user or another sub-system, is a significant factor in the design process since it influences both implementation and subsequent maintenance.

4.8   Things to Think About

* What are the problems of making software machine-dependent?

* What sort of data structures would you use in the design of a time-
  tabling program? You should include in your discussion the invest-
  igative procedure you would adopt in determining its contents. At the
  same time you should describe the individual components and justify
  their inclusion.

* How would you organise a data structure for a database of school
  records? Consideration should be given to the type of information
  held, as well as the amount of information held and its organisation.
  This should be attempted for both BASIC and Pascal implementations.

* Word processor and spreadsheet packages are often provided as standard
  packages on most business microcomputers. Discuss in some detail the
  type of information held, and the data structures that would be best
  suited for the individual applications. Produce a data flow diagram
  reflecting how the data would be used in each case.

* How would you construct a linked-list data structure to hold the names
  and (non-zero) marks of each student in a class? Explore the ways in
  which the structure could be implemented in both BASIC and Pascal, and
  compare the two.

CHAPTER FIVE

Design Methodologies

"It is to be noted that when any part of this paper appears
dull there is a design in it"

Sir Richard Steele, The Tatler No. 38

5.1   Data-orientated Design

There are basically two design approaches which characterise themselves on
the data being manipulated: data flow and data structure design. The
difference between them is reflected in the type of systems for which they
are used. Although it is true to say that they can be applied to the same
environments, there are instances where one approach is better suited to
certain types of application than the other.

Data flow design approaches (Myers(1978) and Yourdon & Constantine (1979))
are most appropriate in situations where there is no apparent structure to
the system data, e.g. in process control environments such as a
nuclear reactor monitoring system. Data structure design (Jackson(1975)
and Warnier(1974)) lends itself more to application areas in which the
data is inherently structured, e.g. in an airline booking system or a
banking system. Although data flow techniques could be used here, it is a
valid argument that a design methodology should take advantage of any
inherent structure in the information that is to be processed may be much
simpler.

Irrespective of the approach taken the resultant software will exhibit a
structure. The nature of the structure is important for it will reflect
the ways in which the identified modules relate to each other. In this
respect, a hierarchical structure is often preferred because it minimises
the complexity of the module interactions and enables the control
relationships between the individual modules to be shown.

A useful analogy towards an appreciation of this abstract concept is that of the hierarchical managerial structures within an organisation - boss, middle management and shop floor workers all relate to software modules which operate more effectively with hierarchy than with anarchy. Certainly it is easier to visualise and effect efficient control procedures so as to ensure that the correct operational processes are enforced if the software exhibits a hierarchical structure.

To be able to achieve this, it is necessary to assume superordinate and subordinate relationships between modules - the general rule of thumb being that a subordinate module may only have one superordinate module, whereas a superordinate module may have many subordinate modules. In this way the mode of operation of a subordinate is dictated by a superordinate. The process of breaking the software down in this way is sometimes called factoring. The resultant hierarchical software structure, illustrated in figure 5.1, is called a structure chart.

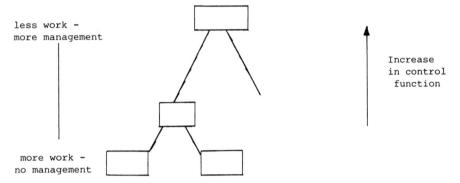

less work -
more management

more work -
no management

Increase
in control
function

Fig 5.1 Structure chart

5.1.1 DATA FLOW DESIGN

Data flow design has its origins within the philosophies of top-down design and structured programming. It has resulted as a natural extension of these ideas by incorporating data flow within the design process. To this extent data flow diagrams are used to show the flow of information within a system, from which a software structure is produced. The method-ology produces, via a data flow diagram, preliminary design of the software structure from the requirement specification.

The process starts by establishing whether the information flow is of a transform or transaction type, since the type of information flow dictates the analytical approach to be taken in producing the software structure. The next step is to determine from the data flow diagram the boundaries which represent a change in the nature of the information - at what stage does the information change from being external to internal, and vice versa. From this, the control hierarchy of the software modules can be determined - the factoring decisions about what operations are to be performed by which modules and in what order. Although the actual form of the structure depends upon the flow category, it is derived from the data flow diagram.

We now consider separately the data flow approach for both transform and transaction flows. Note, however, that irrespective of whether a transform or transaction approach is employed the objective is the same: to define the individual modules and establish the interfaces between them.

5.1.1.1 Transform Analysis

The transform analysis approach is based upon the classification of the data as it passes through the system. For this purpose three data types are defined:

*   Afferent data - incoming data, or data which is transferred from a subordinate to a superordinate module. The transference of data upwards through the hierarchy is said to be performed by an afferent module (figure 5.2).

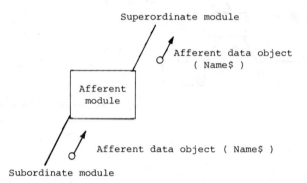

Fig 5.2 Afferent data transfer

*   Efferent data - data which is destined for the outside world, or data that is transferred from a superordinate to a subordinate module. The transference of data down through the hierarchy is said to be performed by an efferent module (figure 5.3).

*   Transform data - data objects which are solely concerned with the transformation of a data object from one form to another. A module which solely performs this function is called a transform module. Although the discussion of afferent and efferent modules have been based upon them passing the data object unchanged, a more likely situation is that they will actually transform the data items in some way (figure 5.4).

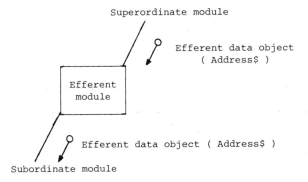

Fig 5.3 Efferent data transfer

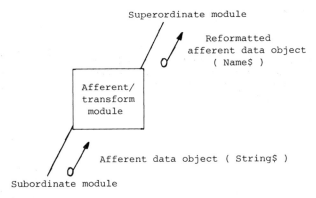

Fig 5.4 Afferent transformation

Having produced a data flow diagram and determined that transform flow is being dealt with, the steps in producing a software structure are thus:

* Identify afferent and efferent flow boundaries.

* Determine the general software structure whilst considering the distribution of the control functions; figure 5.5 gives a generic view of
  the software structure.

* Perform a refinement in the form of a second level of factoring by a
  mapping of the individual bubbles in the data flow diagrams onto
  corresponding modules; figure 5.6 illustrates this process.

* Continually refine the structure until a sufficient level of detail
  is achieved. Design heuristics for conducting this sort of refinement
  are outlined in section 5.5 below.

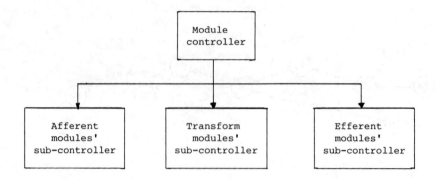

Fig 5.5 General software structure

5.1.1.2 Transaction Analysis

In some systems the arrival of certain data items results in one of a number of alternative data processing paths being chosen - for example, a menu is presented to a user who responds with a keyword which determines not only which data objects are processed but also the nature of that processing. This is depicted in figure 5.7.

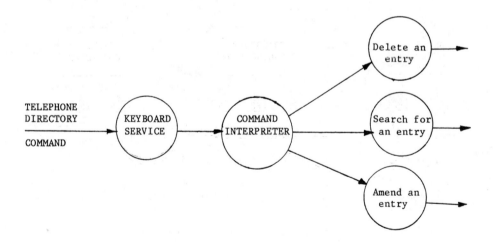

Fig. 5.7   Alternative Data Processing Paths

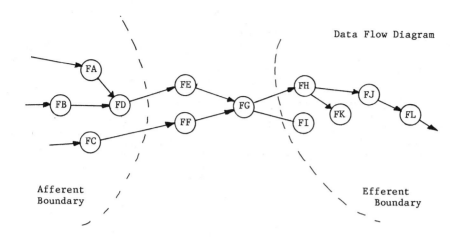

Data Flow Diagram

Afferent
Boundary

Efferent
Boundary

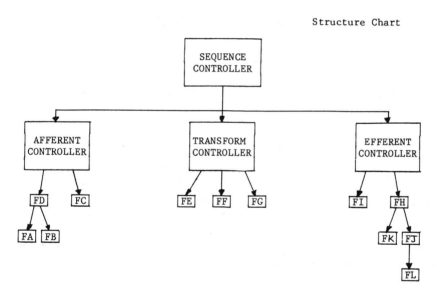

Structure Chart

Fig. 5.6   Mapping of Data Flow to Modules

A data item which triggers such a selection function is called a transaction. In transaction analysis data arrives from the outside world via a
reception path and is converted into its internal format before being
passed onto the transaction centre. This data is then used by the transaction centre to select and initiate one of a number of alternative
processing paths (or action paths as they are sometimes called). The
transaction centre is considered to be the focal point of the control
software, lying between the reception and processing paths.

Having produced a data flow diagram and determined that transaction flow
is being dealt with, the steps in producing a software structure are thus:

* Determine the transaction centre and the flow characteristics of each
  processing path. Produce a software structure from the data flow
  diagram which fits in with the role of the transaction centre. It may
  be viewed generically as shown in figure 5.8.

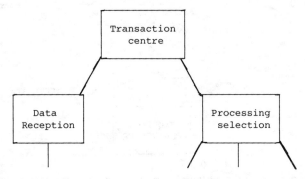

Fig. 5.8 Generic view of software structure

* Determine the software structure for each aspect from the data flow
  diagram, by translating the bubbles into modules; figure 5.9 illustrates this process.

* Continually refine the structure until a sufficient level of detail
  is achieved. Design heuristics for conducting this sort of refinement
  are outlined in section 5.5 below.

With this approach the intention is not only to produce well-defined data
structures, but also well-defined modules and interfaces.

5.1.1.3 HYBRID APPROACH

It is possible to have an analytical approach which incorporates both
transaction and transform techniques. For example, in a large system it
may be prudent to analyse the data reception path and produce a software
structure on an afferent data flow basis. It may also prove to a worth-
while exercise to analyse the various processing paths and produce a

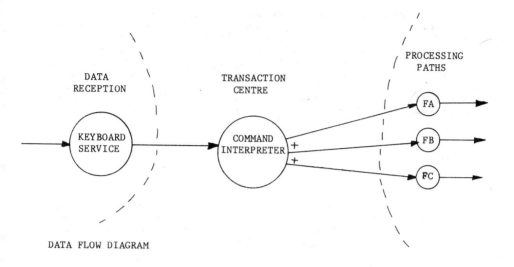

DATA FLOW DIAGRAM

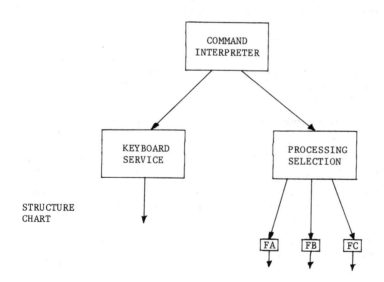

STRUCTURE
CHART

Fig. 5.9   Translation of Data Flow Diagram
into Software Structure

software structure from the viewpoint of an efferent data flow.

There is no simple answer to the question as to what is the best approach. It is simply a matter of choosing the approach which you believe to be the best suited for the application under consideration. All the information surrounding the design, and the rationale behind the adoption of a given software structure, should be supplied in the supporting documentation. The documentation should include such information as the data structures used, the functions of the various individual modules, the hierarchical relationship between the modules, the interfaces between them, and so on. This way you cannot fail!

5.1.2 DATA STRUCTURE DESIGN

Data structure design methodologies aim to produce a software structure based on the data structure which that software is to manipulate. In this way the intention is to produce a procedural description of the software structure which reflects the hierarchical representation of the data structure.

There are a number of data structure design methodologies in existence including Jackson(1975) and Warnier(1974), with Jackson being the most popular. Each has its own set of rules which differ, of course; however each performs the following basic set of tasks:

* Evaluate the characteristics of the data structures.

* Determine the internal format of the various data structures, in par-ticular the relationships between the various constituents of that structure. In this way it is possible to determine sequences, selec-tion and repetition between the elements.

* Construct a software control hierarchy which reflects the data structure.

* Refine the software chart using the guidelines as provided by the adopted methodology.

* Produce a procedural description of the software in a program format using some form of pseudo-code - a 'pidgin' programming language.

The remainder of this section will be devoted to a description of Jackson Structured Programming (JSP) methodology.

Jackson's methodology is a data structure design technique which ident-ifies three basic structural forms - sequence, condition and repetition. A graphical notation is used to define the data structure, which is then used in conjunction with a set of transformation procedures to produce the software structure.

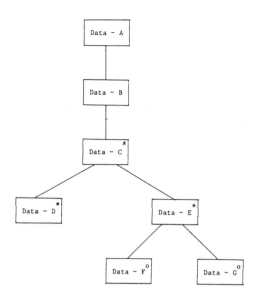

Fig. 5.10   JSP Notation

The notation is shown by the example in figure 5.10. There, two special symbols are used; '*' denotes repetition and 'o' denotes a condition. Data structure Data_A comprises a sub-structure called Data_B (one might argue that this is a trivial example, and one would be right!), which in turn comprises a number of multiple occurrences of sub-structure Data_C, which itself comprises of multiple occurrences of Data_D and one occurrence of Data_E. Data_E contains either Data_F or Data_G.

Let us illustrate the translation of such a data structure into a procedural specification by way of an example. Consider the following data file for use in determining the total salary and tax payments made by a company. Information is held on a project number basis:

```
Project No. XXXX
    Pay code 1
            Overtime
            Tax code
            Salary paid this month
            Tax paid this month
    Pay code 2
          |
          |
    Pay code n
          |
          |
```

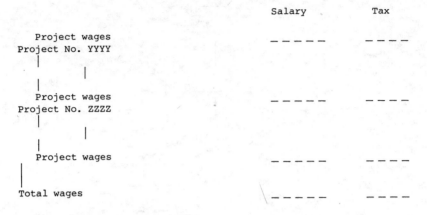

	Salary	Tax
Project wages	————	————
Project No. YYYY		
Project wages	————	————
Project No. ZZZZ		
Project wages	————	————
Total wages	————	————

The first step would be to translate this information into a data structure (figure 5.11) reflecting the relationships between the data items.

Next, the data structure is translated (figure 5.12) into what is called a
procedural representation.

Once the program has been specified in this form it can then be easily
translated into a procedural specification of the program using pseudo-
code.

```
Proc_Pay_Acc -
        open payroll file
        |
        repeat Project_Group -
                Proc_Project_Code; { obtain project number }
                repeat Proc_Pay_Details
                        { obtain overtime, tax code, calculate
                          salary and tax for this month }
                for all Pay_Codes;
                Proc_Wages;
        for all Project_No;
        Total_Wages -
                Proc_Total_Salary;
                Proc_Total_Tax;
        end of ToTal_Wages;
    end of Proc_Pay_Acc;
```

Note that Jackson's method moves directly to procedural constructs like
sequence, condition and repetition without going via a data flow diagram
to a software structure chart.

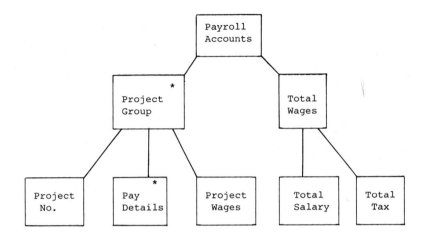

Fig 5.11 Payroll example: data structure

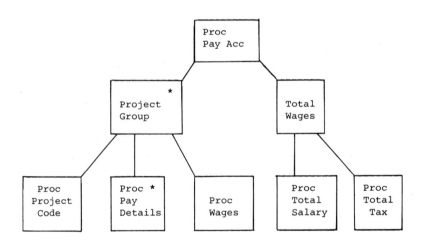

Fig 5.12 Payroll example: procedural representation

91

5.2 Functional Design

Functional design (or top-down stepwise refinement), one of a collection of top-down approaches proposed by Wirth(1971), is a programming technique based upon the philosophy of 'divide and conquer'. One of the earliest methods used to organise programs in a structured way, the general approach is to begin by specifying a program as a series of functional steps such as:

1. REPEAT
2. Obtain user response.
3. Select appropriate action as defined by user response.
4. Present results to the user.
5. UNTIL The End.

The next stage is to take each of the statements in turn and refine them so as to provide a slightly more detailed functional description:

1. REPEAT
2. Obtain user response.
   2.1 Present user with a menu.
   2.2 Read user response.
3. Select appropriate action as defined by user response.
   3.1 IF response is to modify a record then ....
   3.2 ELSE IF the response is to delete a record then .....
   3.3 ELSE IF ......

4. Present results to the user.
   4.1 ....

5. UNTIL The End.
   5.1 UNTIL an exit command is received.

Even from such a simple program section both the functional characterist-ics and the program structure are becoming clearer. The results of the next stage would look something like:

1. REPEAT
2. Obtain user response.
   2.1 Present user with a menu.
      2.1.1 Print_Menu;
   2.2 Read user response.
      2.2.1 READ (User_Response);
3. Select appropriate action as defined by user response.
   3.1 IF response is to modify a record then ....
      ELSE IF the response is to delete a record then .....
      ELSE IF ......
      3.1.1   CASE User_Response OF
              Modify : Amend_Record (Record_Entry);
              Delete : Delete_Record (Record_Entry);

```
        END { of CASE command selection }
        OTHERWISE : Print_Error ( Message );

  3.1.2
  3.1.3
4. Present results to the user.
  4.1 .............
        4.1.1 Print_Results ( Data_value );
        4.1.2
        4.1.3
5. UNTIL The End.
    5.1 UNTIL an exit command is received.
        5.1.1 UNTIL User_Response = Exit;
```

The functional decomposition would continue in this way until the individual statements were expressed in terms of a particular programming language. It is worth noting that even in the above code separate modules are beginning to be specified, e.g. Amend_Record and Print_Error. As a consequence the functional characteristics of individual sub-programs are emerging, as are the data structures upon which they operate. It is believed that a natural structure to both the data and the software will emanate from this process of decomposition.

Note that during each iteration of this decomposing process a number of design decisions are made. Consequently it is essential that the designer is aware of all the alternative solutions (e.g. whether to use a succession of IFs or a CASE statement), and ensure that the choice is not only justified but also documented. This is equally important for data, where the type and format of the individual items should be recorded.

Although stepwise refinement appears to be a self-documenting approach there is a danger that the highest levels of specification may become outdated as program changes are effected at the lower levels of abstraction. Supporting documentation is particularly important and needs to be continually reviewed and updated so as to keep in step with any alterations in program design.

The generic structure of the software is to have a control program which acts as a sequencer for the individual actions. At the higher levels the actions are normally specified in procedural terms. Their effectuation is achieved through sub-programs which eventually decompose down into coded units.

This early top-down design approach is visibly a forerunner of the data flow design techniques that have been discussed above. Other earlier work on the decomposition of procedural definitions of programs in a modular fashion was called structured programming. Dijkstra(1972) formalised the design of software using three basic constructs (sequence, condition, and repetition) in an attempt to minimise the complexity a of the resultant structure. Parnas(1972) described a set of guidelines for the decomposition of a program into a number of sub-programs. These guidelines aimed to formalise the specification of modules by identifying their function directly, rather than via a flowchart. Furthermore, data used within a

93

module which did not need to be known by another module should be 'hidden' (i.e. declared within the module). This not only reduces any confusion over what a module needs to know, but also distinguishes between internal data and any external interface data. In order to minimise the complexity of the interfaces Parnas argued that as little information as possible should be included in a module's interface specification. These aspects - module cohesion and module coupling - are discussed further in section 5.4 below.

5.3   Control Structures in Basic and Pascal

Design methodologies, as we have seen, produce software designs which all assume mechanisms for the programming of conditions and repetitions. For this reason the software designer needs to be aware of what is possible in terms of prorammi‍ng language capabilities; in this section we look at the relevant bits of BBC BASIC and Pascal and assess their respective merits.

The control flow through a program would, without any interference, go straight from the first executable statement through to the last. In any non-trivial program, however, there are a number of points at which decisions are made which determine the instruction path to be followed next. Consequently there is a need to have instructions - control constructs - which enable decisions to be made and alternative program paths to be selected. It is important from a software engineering viewpoint that all such decisions are clearly identifiable, and that all the alternative program paths are clearly marked.

In what follows, a number of the control constructs in BASIC and Pascal are presented and comparatively assessed. Note that when a 'statement' in Pascal is mentioned, it may be either a single statement, or a number of statements enclosed between BEGIN and END to form what is known as compound statement. In BBC BASIC no strictly comparable facility is available, although a number of statements may be placed on one line by separating them with colons (:).

5.3.1 IF STATEMENT

Early versions of BASIC had a simple format for the IF statement, namely

        IF <condition> THEN <linenumber>

which simply meant that if the condition were TRUE then control would be transfered to the instruction at linenumber - in effect, an implicit GOTO statement. BBC BASIC has a little more sophistication, its IF statement being of the form:

        IF <condition> THEN <statement> ELSE <statement>

The severe restriction of having to branch to another part of the program to execute an instruction has been removed. The actual statement(s) may be placed directly in the IF statement, with the statement(s) following THEN being selected if the condition is TRUE and the statement(s) following ELSE if not. It is worth noting that the ELSE part is optional and may be omitted.

    e.g.

    35 IF X_coord > Y_coord THEN Fact = Y_coord: Z_coord = 0

    45 IF Name$ = 'Smythe' THEN Flag% = 2 ELSE Flag% = 1: Index% = 4

    90 IF (X_coord - Y_coord) < 0 THEN PRINT Z ELSE PRINT " ERROR "

In Pascal the IF statement has the following structure

    IF condition THEN statement(s) ELSE statement(s);

or alternatively

    IF condition THEN statement(s);

The effect is similar to that achieved in BASIC, but with the flexiblity offered in program layout alternative strategies are more apparent:

    BEGIN

    IF X_coord < Y_coord
    THEN   BEGIN   { selected if condition is true }
                Fact := Y_coord;
                Index := 0;
            END { a ';' after the END would cause an error }
    ELSE   BEGIN   { selected if condition is false }
                Fact := X_coord;
                Index := 3;
            END;

    END.

5.3.2 GOTO STATEMENT

The GOTO statement will be introduced before we go into details about why it should carry a program health warning.

In BASIC the GOTO statement has the form,

```
        GOTO      line number
```

and may be used in stand-alone mode or incorporated within an IF

```
   e.g.    45  IF Index% < 7 THEN Error$ = "Out of bounds" : GOTO 90

                      |


       110  GOTO 50
```

Using line numbers to identify the destination address makes the task of following the control flow relatively easy. On the other hand because the destinations do not have to be explicitly declared they become to easy to use, resulting in a plethora of GOTO statements - which is when problems begin.

In Pascal the format of the GOTO is similar to that of its counterpart in BASIC, with the exception that destination references are labels - which can be numeric or alphanumeric. The main difference is that all labels used have to be explicitly declared in a label declaration section just after the program header:

```
        PROGRAM Test ( Input, Output );

        LABEL
            Exception_handler;

        VAR
            Error_condition : BOOLEAN;
            Status : INTEGER;
                |

        BEGIN
                |

            IF Error_condition THEN
            BEGIN
                Status := 17;
                GOTO Exception_handler;
            END;


                |

        Exception_handler:

                |

        END.
```

Identification of labels in this way at least acts as some sort of control by ensuring that the addition of a new label has to be done explicitly with careful planning and purpose,

BUT .....

For a disciple of any structured approach to software development, the use of GOTO statements is tantamount to heresy. Their use, almost obligatory in older versions of languages such as BASIC and FORTRAN, is never, ever, recommended for the simple reason that GOTO statements effectively destroy the structure of a program. Trying to follow a control sequence, or trace a fault, in a program littered with GOTO statements is rather like looking for a needle in a haystack which is stored in the middle of a maze. Treat GOTO statements as you should alcohol: the odd one might not do any untold harm, but the more you have the less likely you are to know what's going on.

The use of a GOTO statement should be the exception rather than the rule - as good a way as any to indicate that one of the few justifiable uses of the GOTO is in the implementation of a program's error handling routines in those languages in which no formal error exception handling facilties are provided. In such cases, the Pascal example above, combining IF and GOTO statements serves an isolated, and reasonably well-defined, purpose.

5.3.3 FOR STATEMENT

There are many situations which require the repeated execution of the same sequence of instructions on identical data components, such as the initialisation of every element of an array - a requirement that the FOR statement is designed to meet.

In BASIC the FOR statement has the following format:

FOR control variable = initial value TO final value STEP step value
|
statement(s)
|
NEXT control variable

The control variable is set to the initial value, being incremented therafter by the step value until it exceeds the final value. The sequence of instructions following the FOR statement, up to the corresponding NEXT statement, are executed for every value of the control variable. The initial and final values may themselves be variables or expressions which are determined at run time. The control variable may be of any numeric type, i.e. real or integer, but must not be altered by any instruction enclosed within the FOR - NEXT structure. The STEP value is optional, and if omitted is assumed to be 1. If included it may be either positive or negative, integer or real.

From a software engineering viewpoint, one of the major disadvantages of FOR statements in BASIC is that it is not immediately obvious which instructions belong to any particular FOR, especially when they are nested. Proper indentation of those instructions belonging to individual FOR statements can assist in this area. Another annoying thing about FOR statements in BASIC is that they can only be used with numeric variables and values - you will see why in a minute!

In Pascal the FOR statement is very similar to the BASIC version apart
from the absence of the step value. The FOR loop increment is restricted
to either +1 or -1 represented by reserved words TO and DOWNTO respectively. Its general format is:

FOR control variable := initial value TO/DOWNTO final value DO statement;

Since the control variable may be INTEGER, CHARACTER or a user-defined
type, the following are all perfectly legal:

```
FOR Index_value := 10 DOWNTO 1 DO
FOR Character_data := 'a' TO 'z' DO
FOR Item := Cycle TO Bat DO
```

The ability to associate user-defined types with repetition is very
attractive since it maintains the consistency of design through from data
analysis. Furthermore, the use of BEGIN and END not only makes the task of
identifying which instructions belong to a FOR statement that much
easier, but also clearly identifies the functional characteristics of that
program segment. The following example tries to illustrate how Pascal's
structuring affords both functional visibility and visibility of
association between instructions.

```
CONST
    X_first = -5;
    X_last = 5;
    Y_first = 1;
    Y_last = 10;

TYPE
    X_type : X_first .. X_last;
    Y_type : Y_first .. Y_last;

VAR
    X_coord : X_type;
    Y_coord : Y_type;
    Plot_results : ARRAY [ X_type, Y_type ] OF REALS;
              |

BEGIN
                  |

    FOR X_coord := X_first TO X_last DO
        FOR Y_coord := Y_first TO Y_last DO
        BEGIN
                  |
            WRITE( Plot_results [ X_coord, Y_coord ] );
                              { print the X/Y coordinate value }
                  |
        END;
                  |
    END.
```

5.3.4 CASE/ON STATEMENTS

It is often a requirement that during the execution of a program one of a
number of possible instructions be chosen as a result of some previous
calculation. Sound software engineering depends on a programming language
providing what is very attractive programming facility whilst ensuring
that the resultant code has adequate structure and functional clarity.

In BASIC this 'multiple-choice' facility is provided by the ON statement,
which has the general form:

            ON on-variable GOTO line-1, line-2, .. line-N

where line 1, line 2, etc. represent the line numbers of the instructions
to which control is to be transferred. The line actually chosen depends
upon the numeric value of the on-variable: if it is 1 then control is
transfered to the statement at line-1, if the value is 2 then line-2, and
so on. Basically this is a shorthand method for the more long-winded, but
traditional approach of:

            IF on-value = 1 THEN line-1
            IF on-value = 2 THEN line-2
                    |
            IF on-value = N THEN line-N

The possibility of an on-value being generated which is out range, i.e.
not having a corresponding line number, can be avoided by the inclusion of
an ELSE clause,

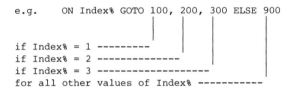

        e.g.   ON Index% GOTO 100, 200, 300 ELSE 900
                              | | | |
        if Index% = 1 -------- | | |
        if Index% = 2 -------------- | |
        if Index% = 3 ------------------- |
        for all other values of Index% ----------

Whilst the ON statement in BASIC does provide the multi-path capability we
are looking for, it certainly does little to assist with the maintenance
of a good program structure, since it is not at all clear from the instruction which part corresponds to which action. Given its reliance on GOTO
(or GOSUB) as an integral element of the instruction, and the difficulties
that that poses, it might be argued that ON should be turned off.

The equivalent instruction in Pascal is the CASE statement which has the
general format:

        CASE selector OF
            option 1 : statement(s);
            option 2 : statement(s);
            option 3 : statement(s);
                    |
        END
        OTHERWISE : statement(s); {OTHERWISE is optional}

The selector may be an integer or character variable, or it may be a user-defined type. The example below illustrates the use of CASE in producing displayed output related to a user-defined type (which is an abstract entity, remember). Although the coding looks somewhat cumbersome, the structure is sound and functional clarity maintained in a way that, say, use of the ON statement in BASIC would not.

```
    TYPE
        Object = ( Cycle, Ball, Car, Book, Doll, Bat );

    VAR
        Item : Object;

    BEGIN
                |

        Item := Ball; { an assignment to Item }
        WRITE ( 'The item sold was a ' ); { first part of the
                                                output message }
        CASE Item OF
            Cycle : WRITELN ( ' cycle. ' );
            Ball :  WRITELN ( ' ball. ' );
            Car :   WRITELN ( ' car. ' );
            Book :  WRITELN ( ' book. ' );
            Doll :  WRITELN ( ' doll. ' );
            Bat :   WRITELN ( ' bat. ' );
        END;
        WRITELN ( ' Payment was made in cash. ' );

                |

    END.
```

5.3.5 REPEAT STATEMENT

A characteristic, which often becomes an inconvenience, of FOR statements is that the number of repetitions is fixed on entry to the loop. In cases where a forced exit is required during the repetitive execution of the loop an IF statement may be used. In 'older' languages like FORTRAN and BASIC this was the only of performing this activity:

```
e.g.                |
        30  Function = Test * Xcoord
        40  FOR I = 1 TO 15
        50  If I > 8 THEN GOTO 85
                    |
        85  IF Function > 25.6 THEN GOTO 150
        90  Array ( I ) = I * Function
```

100

```
 95 Function = Test * Xcoord
100 NEXT I
    |
150 PRINT ' Function value = '; Function
    |
```

Although this approach works it is not clear which IF statement(s) are associated with particular exit conditions, as opposed to those that are there as part of the algorithmic sequence. As a result of this confusion it is not clear which IFs need to be altered to effect a change in the exit conditions for a particular loop.

A development within BBC BASIC - the REPEAT - clearly depicts the exit conditions for a sequence of statememts. It formally specifies the exit conditions for a particular repetition sequence by enclosing them between REPEAT and a terminating 'UNTIL condition', thus:

```
        REPEAT
           |
        statement(s)
           |
        UNTIL condition(s)
```

The sequence of statements is repeatedly executed until the condition is TRUE. Note that the sequence is always executed at least once as the exit test appears at the end of the statement(s).

e.g.

```
 45 Index% = 0
 50 Function = Test_value * X_coord
 55 IF Function > 25.6 THEN GOTO 120
 60 REPEAT
 70 Index% = Index% + 1
    |
 90 Array ( Index% ) = Index% * Function
100 Function = Test_value * X_coord
110 UNTIL ( Index% = 15 ) OR ( Function > 25.6 )
120 IF Function > 25.6 THEN PRINT " Function = "; Function
    |
```

From a software engineering viewpoint it is much easier to see the conditions under which that sequence of instructions will cease. Indeed it is easy to see where one should make the appropriate alterations to effect different exit conditions, especially where nested REPEAT instructions are used.

The functional characteristics of the REPEAT instruction in Pascal are identical, the format of the statement being:

```
        REPEAT
           |
        statement(s);
           |
        UNTIL exit condition(s);
```

The use of BEGIN - END to bracket the statements to be REPEATed is not neccesary since the grouping is defined by the statement's enclosure between the reserved words REPEAT and UNTIL.

```
      CONST
           Max_index = 15;
           Max_value = 25.6;

      VAR
           Function, X_coord, Test_value : REAL;
           Index : INTEGER;
           Data_set : ARRAY [ 1 .. Max_index ] OF REAL;

      BEGIN

           Function := Test_value * X_coord; { initialise Function }
           IF Function > Max_value
              THEN  WRITELN (' Function = ', Function)
              ELSE
              BEGIN
                   Index := 0; { initialise array index }
                   REPEAT

                       Index := Index + 1; { increment array index }
                       Data_set [ Index ] := Index * Function;
                       Function := Test_value * X_coord;
                   UNTIL (Index = Max_index) OR (Function > Max_value);
                   IF Function > 25.6 THEN WRITELN (' Function = ',
                                                             Function);

              END; { of the ELSE clause }

    END.
```

Here, the inherent structure of Pascal adds to that of the REPEAT facility to enhance the general understandability of the program code - which, of course, is a primary objective of software engineering.

5.3.6 WHILE STATEMENT

The WHILE statement is an alternative Pascal control construct which is not available in BBC BASIC. WHILE is intended to complement REPEAT, by catering for those situations in which having to use a statement that tests for exit at the end of the instruction sequence would be inconvenient.

The Pascal REPEAT example, above, illustrates both the problem and the way in which the program design is affected if a WHILE facility is absent. There, the necessity to test the value of Function prior to entry, just in case it is not already greater than Max_value, adds a level of complexity to the program structure. It is such situations, provoked by the fact that REPEATs are always executed once, that WHILE is designed to meet.

The general form of the WHILE statement is:

        WHILE <condition> DO <statement(s)>;

its effect being to execute the statementsonly if condition is true: an entry test, as opposed to the exit test of REPEAT. Consequently care must be taken to ensure that the requisite conditions are set to effect exit at the appropriate time, and that the relevant variables are updated at the correct place within the overall sequence in respect to the test conditions.

The example below is the program part of the REPEAT example of 5.3.5, modified to incorporate a WHILE statement.

```
    BEGIN
                  |
        Index := 0; { initialise array index }
        Function := Test_value * X_coord;
        WHILE ( Index < Max_index ) AND ( Function < Max_value ) DO
            BEGIN
                      |
                Index := Index + 1; { increment array index }
                Data_set [ Index ] := Index * Function;
                Function := Test_value * X_coord;
            END;
        IF Function > Max_value THEN WRITELN(' Function = ', Function);
                  |
    END.
```

There are two things to notice from a software engineering viewpoint: Firstly the overall structure is easier to understand and actually uses fewer statements than the REPEAT version. Secondly, the individual exit conditions have been changed along with the OR for an AND. As a guideline, where it is important to test at the end of the sequence then a REPEAT will normally be used; if a test needs to be performed on entry to an instruction sequence then a WHILE is usually more appropriate. Care must be taken when changing from one to the other, both in terms of instruction sequence and setting exit conditions.

5.4   Module Decomposition

The organisation of a computer program can be likened to that of a large company. If everyone reported directly to the managing director then nothing would get done; chaos and confusion would reign. A company organisation which is structured (factored) will operate more efficiently and effectively than one that isn't, with the many organisational procedures distributed amongst the line management team rather than loaded onto one key person.

In the same way, a modular approach to software design and construction enhances program efficiency and effectiveness. Decomposing a program into a number of modules which operate together produces manageable entities; representing the program structure in a hierarchic manner minimises the complexity of the overall design, making analysis that much easier.

The production of a hierarchic sofware chart enables the software engineer to analyse the individual modules and their characteristics. Based on such a chart, various principles have evolved which guide the effectiveness of this analytical process at any stage of refinement during software development. A description of these guidelines is given below.

5.4.1 SOFTWARE STRUCTURE

A software structure chart (as shown in figure 5.13) is used to show the hierarchic relationships of the individual modules. The visibilty offered permits the overall design to be 'measured' by certain metrics to see how good the design actually is. Generally speaking the metrics are aimed at the control aspect of the structure rather than any functional considerations. There are basically four metrics which can be used on data directly accessible from the software chart. It should be remembered that there are not fixed rules, they should only be used as guidelines. These metrics are:

Fan In - a measure of the number of superordinate modules that
control a subordinate module.

Fan Out - a measure of the number of subordinate modules that are
controlled by a given superordinate.

Depth - the number of levels in the overall structure.

Width - the maximum number of modules which result at any given
level.

If these values are minimised, then the overall effect on the resultant software will that of reduced complexity.

5.4.2 INFORMATION HIDING

Module testing and integration becomes easier when the amount of information that is needed to be known by the producer of any individual module is kept to a minimum. This principle (suggested by Parnas(1972)), termed information hiding, decrees that the information held within a module should be inaccesible to other modules unless specified. The intention is to effect a modular structure by designing a set of independent modules which communicate only that information which is

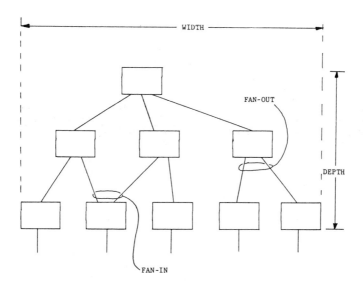

Fig. 5.13   Structure Chart

necessary to effect the overall software function.

5.4.3 MODULE INDEPENDENCE

Simplifying the functionality of each of the modules, and their respective interfaces, significantly simplifies the tasks of fault diagnosis, software verification and testing, and maintenance. Designing modules which exhibit the characteristics of performing a single task, and have simple interfaces with other modules, clearly reduces the software engineer's psychiatric bills.

Two criteria have been identified to assisst in the qualitative assessment of module independence: coupling and cohesion.

5.4.3.1 Coupling

Coupling is a measure of the interdependence between superordinate and subordinate modules. Coupling depends upon the complexity of the interfaces between modules: how they are called and how the data is passed between them. The intention is to design for coupling which is as low as possible - in other words, high module independance.

Figure 5.14 reflects the conclusions of Myers(1978), who identified seven
levels of coupling, as follows (in decreasing order of desirability):

* Content - one module uses the data that is local to another.

* Common - two or more modules share a global common data region.
  [This was (and indeed still is) the most frequently used technique for
  transferring data items between FORTRAN subprograms]

* External - two or modules share a non-common global data region.

* Control - one module passes a ' flag ' to another which will determine
  the subordinate module's run-time behaviour.

* Stamp - as common coupling, except that data elements are passed
  between modules as parameters.

* Data - one module passes data directly to another via a parameter list
  [In this way the subordinate module performs its allotted function on
  the data items supplied in the parameter list. Every attempt should be
  made to keep the parameter list as small as possible]

* No coupling - totally independent modules

5.4.3.2 Cohesion

Ideally, a cohesive module will perform a single task on the data objects
supplied. Again (see figure 5.15) Myers(1979) has identified seven types of
cohesion (in decreasing order of desirability):

Coincidental - modules perform a number of tasks which have no association between them.

Logical - modules perform one of a set of tasks as selected by the
calling module.

Classical - modules perform multiple sequential functions which have
some association.

Procedural - modules perform a number of functions as defined by the
application.

Communication - as procedural cohesion except that data items are
passed along the sequence and used in each function.

Functional - a module performs only one task

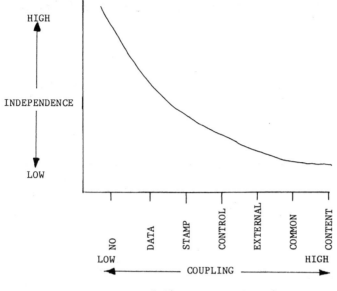

Fig. 5.14   Module Coupling

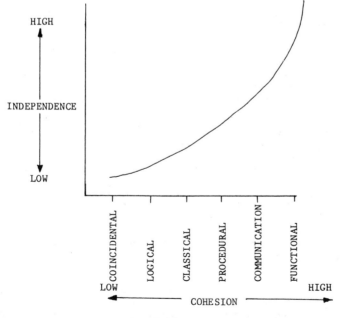

Fig. 5.15   Module Cohesion

5.5 Procedures and Functions in Basic and Pascal

The principles of module decomposition can only be put into practice if programming languages provide the necessary support. In this section we look at the offerings of BBC BASIC and Pascal in this respect, and their consequent influence on software design.

In general terms we will be discussing subprograms, defined as recogniseable pieces of self-contained code the precise operation of which is determined by data supplied to it at run-time.

In early versions of BASIC the only form of subprogram was implemented using the GOSUB statement, the function of which is to transfer control to the subprogram whose first instruction is identified by the line number in the GOSUB statement. The end of the subprogram is identified by a RETURN statement which returns control to the statement following the GOSUB.

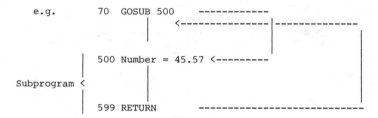

It is possible in some later versions of BASIC to incorporate the ON and the GOSUB statements so as to select one of a number of GOSUB options:

ON on-variable GOSUB line-1, line-2, ... line-N

Such a highly-informal approach to the construction of modules means that a disciplined development procedure is difficult to enforce. There are a number of software engineering nasties associated with the use of GOSUBs:

* They only operate on global variables, which makes it very difficult to see exactly what is being operated on by the subprogram. As a consequence, the detection of any deliberate or accidental corruption of the global variables is very hard to pin down. This invariably means that when an error is detected in a subprogram the whole program comes under scrutiny.

* the direct interaction between main program and subprograms makes it impossible to test the different parts of the program indepenently.

* the only form of identification being the line number, the enforcement of <u>any</u> sort of structure is impossible: in fact any line number could be the entry point to a subroutine!

In addition to GOSUB, BBC BASIC also has a mechanism for the declaration of procedures and functions. Generally speaking a procedure is a collection of instructions which, when called into action, perform a specific activity on the set of data values supplied with any results produced by the procedure being returned to the calling(usually the main) program via defined variables. A function on the other hand actually produces a single result which is returned to the calling program via the name of the function. Both functions and procedure can have variables declared within them which are local to them.

5.5.1 PROCEDURES

In BBC BASIC procedures are usually declared at the end of the main program using a statement of the form:

        DEF PROCname (parameter list)

where the parameter list is optional. All statements enclosed between DEFPROC and the corresponding

        ENDPROC

statement are associated with that procedure. The procedure is invoked simply by quoting its name:

        PROCname

On return from that procedure the instruction following the PROCname will be executed. Parameters are uni-directional in BASIC, i.e. they may be used to feed data values to a procedure but cannot be used to transport the values back to the main program. Values to be returned to the main program have to be associated with global variables.

Consider a program in which it is required to sort the values in an array, Alpha, into ascending order. It is assumed for simplicity that the array has a maximum of 10 elements. The program below performs this function, inefficiently, using a procedure to perform the test-and-swap function.

```
         |
    30   FOR Index% = 1 TO 9
    45   PROCascending ( Alpha ( Index% ), Alpha ( Index% + 1 ) )
    50   Alpha ( Index% ) = Lower
    55   Alpha ( Index% + 1 ) = Upper
    60   NEXT Index%
         |
    90   END
         |
   100   DEF PROCascending ( First, Last )
   110   LOCAL Temp
   120   IF First > Last THEN Temp = First: First = Last: Last = Temp
   130   Lower = First
   140   Upper = Last
   150   ENDPROC
         |
```

The procedure has two 'formal parameters', First and Last, passed to it as values to be compared. Temp is declared local to the procedure and its value is not known outside of it. Lower and Upper are two global variables which are used to pass back the resultant sorted values. In the main program Alpha(Index%) and Alpha(Index%+1) are passed to the procedure, and are known as 'actual parameters'. The resultant values have to be assigned to the respective array elements when control is returned back to the main program.

Consider, as another example, the printing of telephone directory entry details - an activity which may be required at numerous places within the program. This may be viewed as a simple exercise which can be isolated within a procedure, the only variables being the name and address which are supplied as parameters:

```
           |
 20  Tele_name$ ( I% )  = " P. J. Smythe "
 30  Tele_address$ ( I% , 1 ) = " 22 Dummy St. "
 40  Tele_address$ ( I% , 2 ) = " LONDON SW1 9ZZ "
           |
 90  PROCprint_entry (Tele_name$ ( I% ), Tele_address$ ( I% , 1 ),
                                        Tele_address$ ( I% , 2 ) )
           |
200  END
           |
500  DEF PROCprint_entry ( Name$, Address1$, Address2$ )
510  PRINT " Current telephone entry is :"
520  PRINT " Name : "; Name$
530  PRINT " Address : "; Address1$ , Address2$
540  ENDPROC
           |
```

Even in these limited examples it can be seen that the program design has some visible links with the products of a structured design methodology such as functional decomposition.

The functional characteristics of procedures in BASIC and Pascal are very similar, the major difference being that in Pascal the structure is more formally defined, being akin to that of the main program. For example, a procedure heading is very similar to that of a program header:

           PROCEDURE name (parameter list)

c.f.   PROGRAM name (input/output list)

Also all variables, labels and types which are local to a procedure are declared within that procedure. Although this may appear to be rather tedious, it does mean that through a formal mechanism both the functional characteristics of the procedure and the data objects which are being operated upon are explicitly defined and localised.

The parameter list declares both the type of the formal parameters and their size; parameters may be of any type, including user defined types.

e.g.

```
      PROCEDURE name ( Index : 1 .. 10; Pointer : Link;
                       X_coord : REAL; Result : 1 ..23 );
```

The parameters may also be bi-directional, i.e. they can be used to pass
data values to a procedure as well as provide a mechanism by which results
may be passed back to the main program. Any variable which is not declared
internally (i.e. locally) or does not appear as a parameter are assumed
to be global to the entire program. From a software engineering viewpoint
the formal specification of the procedure and the data objects upon which
it operates maximises visibility. This in turn makes the code a lot easier
to understand and modify.The Pascal equivalent to the BASIC 'swap' example
above would be:

```
              |
      CONST
          Max_numbers = 10;

      VAR
          Index : 1 .. Max_numbers;
          Alpha : ARRAY [ 1 .. Max_numbers ] OF REAL;

      { NOTE: procedures are declared in VAR section }

      PROCEDURE Ascending ( VAR First, Last : REAL );
          VAR
              Temp : REAL;

          BEGIN
              IF First > Last
              THEN BEGIN
                      Temp := First;
                      First := Last;
                      Last := First;
                  END;
          END; { of procedure }

      BEGIN { main program }
              |

          FOR Index := 1 TO Max_numbers-1 DO
              Ascending ( Alpha [ Index ], Alpha [ Index + 1 ] );

              |
```

From the above example it can be seen that there is no need to copy back
the respective values into the array since this is automatically achieved
via the parameters, thereby reducing the amount of code produced.

Unlike BASIC all procedures have to be declared before they are called,
which is why they are positioned within the declaration section. Obviously
this could present a difficulty if two procedures called each other - for
example, if procedure A calls procedure B, and B calls A, there is no way
of effecting a legal declaration. This is actually a Good Thing, since
potential infinite loops such as this should only be entered into by
design, not by accident. For this reason a special mechanism called

FORWARD has to be specifically employed, thus:

```
                     |

      PROCEDURE A ( ..... ); FORWARD;

      PROCEDURE B ( ..... );
                     |
         BEGIN
            |
            A ( .... );
            |
         END; { of procedure B }

      PROCEDURE A ( ..... );
                     |
         BEGIN
            |
            B ( .... );
            |
         END; { of the full declaration of procedure B }

                     |
```


5.5.2 FUNCTIONS

Functions are similar in format to procedures, but are operationally different in that at least one result must be produced by a function and
returned via the function name. For this reason, functions are are usually
called from within an expression, as are system functions such as COS(x)
and SIN(x).

Functions in BASIC are declared at the end of the program by a statement
of the form:

              DEF FNname (parameters)

All statements enclosed between it and the function assignment statement,

                 = result

form part of the function. The name of the function also determines the
type of the answer,

     e.g.   DEF FNIntercept - would return a real result
            DEF FNIntercept% - would return an integer result
            DEF FNEntry$ - would return a character string.

Variables which are not declared as being parameters are either local or
global. A function which returned the sum of its four real variable parameters would look like:

```
50 Test_data (J) = Factor * FNSummation ( Data (I), J, Vector (K), Xray )
|
90 Result = Result + FNSummation ( Test_data (J), Xray, Test_data (K),
                        Vector ( K + J ) )
|
   END
|
150 DEF FNSummation ( One, Two, Three, Four )
160 Local Temp
170 Temp = One + Two + Three + Four
180 = Temp
```

The identity of the data objects under consideration are all visible, as is the type of result being produced. It is worth mentioning that this function definition could be written on one line as

```
150 DEF FNSummation ( One, Two, Three, Four ) = One + Two + Three + Four
```

Unfortunately when this appears in amongst other text it is not so clear as to the function being performed.

Functions in Pascal also produce a single result which is returned via the function name. The only major difference is that the type of the result must be formally defined, which enables a run-time check to be performed on the results produced. The result produced by a function must be formally assigned to the function name before exiting. Implementation of the above summation function in Pascal would look something like:

```
        FUNCTION Summation ( One, Two, Three, Four : REAL) : REAL;
            VAR
                Temp : REAL;
            BEGIN
                Temp := One + Two + Three + Four;
                Summation := Temp;
            END; { of function declaration }
```

and may be simply called by a statement like:

```
        Answer := Count * Summation (a, b, c, d);
```

All functions are located in the declarations section and, where appropriate, the FORWARD referencing mechanism may be used.Obviously the above definition of Summation could be reduced drastically by removing the declaration of Temp and the assignment to it, with the result being assigned directly to Summation. Although this shorthand is similar to that in BASIC, there still has to be a formal definition of the function and its result. This means that almost at a glance its functional characteristics, and the data it operates on, are evident. A trivial point, perhaps, but knowing where to look also helps considerably.

5.6 Summary

* There are basically two design approaches: data flow, and data structure design. Although they can be applied to the same environments, there are instances where one approach may be preferable.

* Data flow design uses data flow diagrams to show the flow of information within a system to produce a structure chart. Depending on the type of information being processed, a structure chart will be produced as a result of either transaction analysis, or transform analysis.

* Data structure design produces a software structure based on the data structure it is to manipulate.

* Functional design is a programming technique whereby the software is specified, in functional terms, in a series of steps. At each step the functional description is refined until a stage is reached at which coded units can be produced.

* The software engineer needs to be aware of the control constructs that are available in different languages. The programming mechanisms for condition and repetition need to be assessed in terms of effectiveness and efficiency.

* A software structure chart needs to be quantitively and qualitively assessed by means of various metrics; design heuristics which can be used in this respect are: fan-in, fan-out, depth, width, cohesiveness and coupling.

* The software engineer needs to be aware of language facilities for the realisation of modules. The mechanisms provided will affect decisions on such aspects as interfacing between modules and how they are to be tested.

5.7 Things to Think About

* What differences, if any, would there be in structure charts for the telephone directory system produced by both transform and transaction analysis techniques?

* Produce a software design for the telephone directory system using the Jackson Structured Programming technique; how do the results compare with the above?

* Design a suite of mathematical routines for use on a microcomputer. Use the process of stepwise refinement, applying design heuristics at every stage.

CHAPTER SIX

Verification and Testing

"Irrationally held truths may be more harmful
than reasoned errors"

Aldous Huxley, Science and Culture xii
The Coming of Age of the Origin of Species

6.1 The Perspective

In this, the last of the chapters grouped under the section heading of
'Software Design Issues', we shall consider the topics of verification and
testing:

a)   verification that the design is a faithful interpretation of the
     requirements specification;

and

b)   testing of the design implementation in terms of the program code
     modules/units which have been produced.

Now whilst a) might be readily accepted as a subject for discussion at
this stage, is not a consideration of item b), the actual testing of the
developed code, applicable to the next section on 'Implementation Issues'?

The short answer is 'yes' - and 'no'. Yes, testing is an integral part of
the implementation process, and will obviously be referred to again at
that point. But no, a consideration of testing must not, in practice, be
deferred until implementation is under way. Verification and testing must
both be anticipated at the design phase. Some versions of the software
life-cycle actually refer to 'detailed design, code and test' as a self-
contained phase in its own right. Certainly the interrelated nature of
these elements, and the highly iterative manner in which this part of a

project's development is conducted, suggest that testing should be firmly in mind when design is under way.

This argument is supported by the growing acceptance that testing is not about proving that something is error-free, but concerned rather with the detection of errors. E.W. Dijkstra's comment that "testing can only show the presence of bugs, never their absence" leads us on to some definitions which are tinged with realism:

* The objective of a test is to uncover an error.

* Tests are designed so as to maximise the chances of uncovering errors hitherto buried.

* A successful test is one which reveals a previously unknown error.

Given that these are the criteria for testing, it can be seen that the aim of a test is to cause another iteration in the design, code, test cycle. This being the case, we must look during the detailed design phase both at the verification of the current design and - forward - to the manner in which tests on the implementation of that design will be carried out. This aspect, planning to accommodate the dynamic nature of the software development life-cycle, is covered in the final section of the chapter.

Before then we must necessarily look at how the whole business is managed. Management! Bo-ring. Do we have to? Afraid so. Recognising that the process of software development is dynamic in nature is one thing; a whirlpool is dynamic as well, but leads straight down the plughole. Unless the potential whirlpool of software development can be controlled - that is, managed - the end product will disappear in much the same way.

6.2 Configuration Management

6.2.1 PRINCIPLES

The term 'configuration', often related to the boxes which make up the hardware complex of a computer system, actually has the wider definition of embracing all the elements, hardware and software, which comprise the product under development. If this configuration were subject to change, through the development of either new hardware or new software - or, heaven forbid, both - then configuration management would be needed so as to effect control of all such change.

Hardware and software configuration management, not unnaturally, share much in common. Hardware configuration management is, thankfully, beyond the scope of this book; in what follows, therefore, the terms 'configuration' and 'configuration management' should be taken to mean 'software configuration', and 'software configuration management' respectively.

A software configuration has been defined as a set of computer software characteristics described in documentation and realised in code. This configuration evolves during development into a series of baselines, or formal document and code software definitions. As we have seen, however, even as this configuration is developing, it is changing. Software configuration management, then, is concerned with the management of those changes - to documentation and code.

What we are after is 'predictable' software. So, it will lead to a dull life, but software which behaves in a manner that is reliable, and known, is the end result that we seek. Complex software, however, comprising many parts - each of which passes through a number of development iterations - is very much akin to a moving target. But in order to come up with some sort of answer to the classic management enquiry - "How's it going then?" - our target has to at least be capable of being halted temporarily, 'frozen', and the state of the software declared. But at such a point, or baseline, we can only claim to 'know' the software as a whole if we are sure that we know exactly which versions of its constituent parts are actually in use. As a first step then, the constituent parts, the configuration items, have to be identified.

6.2.2 CONFIGURATION ITEMS

Configuration items should be determined as one product of the software design specification phase. Unfortunately, there is no firm rule as to just what should, or should not, be designated a configuration item. As a general rule, however, software configuration items should not span the boundary between computers or independent programs. Thus a data base and its controlling program would each be a configuration item. Also, all independently identifiable programs in a system, even though interaction might take place between them, would each be designated as a configuration item. A configuration item should be regarded as a deliverable entity to which certain functions have been assigned. Selection may be based on its administrative complexity, its technical criticality, or its maintenance criticality.

It is the description of a software configuration item (document or code), at any stage in the life cycle, that must be controlled. Even though several configuration items may constitute the software of a system, from the time that the performance requirements of any one has been defined, that item is subject to the control of all documents peculiar to it.

6.2.3 BASELINES

A baseline is an agreed definition of the current status of a product. As such, it is capable of being changed and/or extended only after approval through some formal change control procedure. As far as software products are concerned the baseline, at least during the early stages of development, will comprise the specification documents which describe the final form of the product; later baselines will add the programs themselves to updated and amended versions of these specifications, and other, documents.

The baselines for a software system are established at particular points in the life-cycle. The points are identified during project planning as those at which a known position for the project can, and must, be defined before further developments can be considered. At intermediate stages, the current status of the software is defined by the previous baseline plus any subsequent changes. This latter point will naturally incorporate all changes which are made as the result of errors being corrected; thus the procedures of error reporting and error correction have to be regarded as an integral part of configuration management.

By way of example, the following would be typical baselines, and baseline products:

* Requirements Specification baseline - the point at which the approved requirements specification document is issued. From this point onwards the document is subject to the due rigours of configuration management control, with no alterations made to it without prior approval.

* Software Design Specification baseline - the point at which the design of the software is regarded as complete; thereafter any changes to the design documentation have to be approved and recorded before they can be implemented.

* Detailed Design Specification baseline - module designs, code versions, test specifications and any test programs: all warrant consideration as configuration items in their own right. Individually and, where they are interrelated, collectively, these items will be associated with a baseline.

* System Integration baseline - the various steps of integration and test will be conducted progressively; as each further element is introduced, a new system baseline is established. Note that in this area, as with detailed design, testing and error correction will inevitably result in many intermediate stages between baselines.

* Operational baseline - the system as brought into production working is defined by this baseline. Subsequent error detection and correction, or changes to the original requirements, are necessarily made with respect to this baseline.

Figure 6.1 (based on an example in EEA(1983)) indicates the applicability of each of the above baselines to a number of typical software config- uration items. Note that when an item is reflected in the establishment of a baseline then that status remains, being altered only by the creation of a subsequent baseline.

BASELINES

x = baseline applicable	Requirements. Spec.	Software Design Spec.	Detailed Design Spec.	System Integration	Operational
Quality Assurance Plan	x	x	x	x	
Configuration Management Plan	x	x	x	x	x
System Requirements Specification	x	x	x	x	x
Software Requirements Specification		x	x	x	x
Module Specifications		x	x	x	x
Database Descriptions		x	x	x	x
Module/Unit Design Descriptions			x	x	x
Source Code Listings			x	x	x
Test Plan		x	x	x	
Test Procedures		x	x	x	x
User Manuals			x	x	x
Source, Object, Executable Code				x	x

Fig 6.1 Configuration items vs Baselines

6.2.4 CONFIGURATION MANAGEMENT OF PROGRAM CODE

The configuration management of program code causes particular problems. At least where documents are concerned changes can be identified, albeit with some difficulty, by eye. When dealing with program code, however, even this check is lost. Identification of code changes, verifying that correct versions of modules have been integrated in a system build, can generate acute problems. A clear presentation of the 'development history' of a piece of software is essential if any evidence is to be available, for instance, to confirm that the correct product has been built and tested.

A control system is thus an essential ingredient in sound configuration management of code. Its essential elements would be:

* software development tools to assist in the production of accurate and relevant listings;

* an unambiguous system of version and revision identification;

* consistent application of library control.

The flowchart of figure 6.2 (derived from DEFSTAN 00-16(1984) illustrates a control system for the correction of an error in a piece of software.

119

Note that the same sort of procedure would need to be followed in the event of a change to the requirements specification during development.

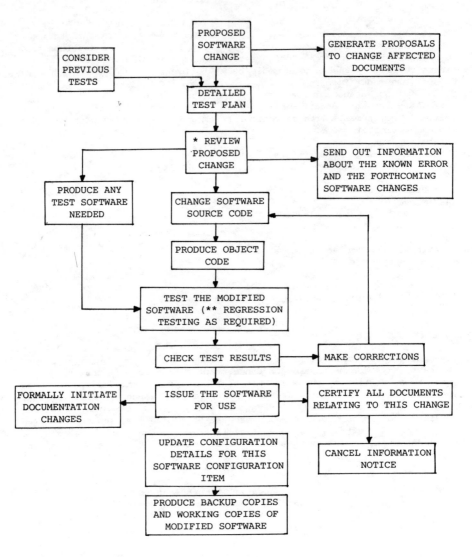

* See 6.3 below
** Repeat earlier tests. See chapter 8

Fig 6.2 Software modification procedure

6.2.5 THE CONFIGURATION MANAGEMENT PLAN

The above should have given an idea of the magnitude of the configuration
management requirement for a major software development project. It should
be accepted without too much argument, therefore, that this aspect demands
a plan of its own - the Configuration Management Plan. Broadly, the main
areas covered by such a plan would be as follows:

* Organisation: identification of the various committees, working groups
  and individuals with responsibilities and/or authority with regard to
  configuration management;

* Documents: specifications, standards, manuals and all other documents
  which must be taken under configuration control;

* Identification: plans for selecting configuration items, maintaining
  specifications and establishing baselines;

* Control: procedures for preparation and submission of change proposals
  for approval, examination of such proposals, implementation of agreed
  changes;

* Audit: procedures for collecting and analysing data for configuration
  accounting purposes;

6.3 The Design Review

"A committee is an animal with four back legs"

George Smiley: Tinker, Tailor, Soldier, Spy.

In which case, let us hope that MI5 never get involved with the software
life-cycle. The principle of review boards for design verification, test
results evaluation, configuration management etc. is proven as a highly
effective method of controlling the development of a software project.

6.3.1 THE ACTIVITY OF DESIGN REVIEW

The design review is not a progress meeting. Rather, its objectives are to
define and control the baselines generated at each phase of the project.
It is essential to ensure that each baseline, as it is created, possesses
credibility. Thus a design review will seek to ensure that the requirements of an immediately preceding baseline have been properly and accurately interpreted by the design under review.

The design review should, almost by virtue of its existence,

* encourage the application of design methodologies, coding conventions and other good practices as defined in the Code of Practice under which the project is being developed;

* provide a means of making a design visible;

* facilitate design audits by providing a traceable path through the design from Requirements Specification to the finished and accepted product;

* enable an assessment to be made of the maturity of the design.

6.3.2 DESIGN REVIEW STRUCTURE

A design review should have a defined input and a defined output - with the qualification, however, that its objective is to evaluate the design under review rather than ask ad hoc questions about it. The following tasks may be identified:

Pre-Review

* Identify membership for the review meeting. Only those personnel who are in a position to make a direct contribution should attend. This is going to depend on the nature of the review, but will usually comprise representatives of the customer, the project team, management, quality assurance.

* Identify documentation needed for the meeting, and circulate it beforehand.

* Clearly state the objectives of the review e.g. 'Approval of the Design Specification for Modules X,Y and Z and agreement to proceed'.

* Ensure the availability of a secretary to keep records at the meeting.

* Arrange any necessary demonstrations.

During the Review

* The design team make a short presentation which relates the design to its previous baseline, and argues that it has met those things required of it.

* Members of the review board then evaluate the design by questioning the design team.

* Questions raised, and answers to them, are recorded.

* Formal decisions should be recorded which indicate that the objectives of the review have, or have not been met: all being well, the meeting will also give formal approval to proceed.

* In either case, any unresolved questions and/or doubtful points should be recorded as actions against nominated individuals with an agreed date for their response.

Post-Review

* Agreed minutes of the review are circulated to all parties concerned.

* Action taken (usually under Configuration Management) to formally issue or control any item approved by the review.

* All actions from the review are followed up (by the Chairperson) in a timely manner.

6.3.3 REVIEW CHECK-LISTS

A check list is a valuable aid towards the evaluation of a design at the review meeting. Such a list will relate to the design level currently under review, and will seek to ensure that:

a) the design is consistent with the approved baseline from any previous review

and

b) overall system design considerations and practices, as encapsulated in a company Code of Practice, for instance, are actually being employed in the development of the project.

It must be remembered, however, that a check-list should serve as an aide-memoire and is not the be-all and end-all of a design review, the objective of which is to evaluate a design, not merely answer a list of questions about it.

By way of example, the following is a representative check-list designed to cover particular levels of review (d=design, dd=detailed design, m=module, u=unit); in practice, of course, this basic list would be tailored and augmented as appropriate to the software project in question.

* Actions - have actions from previous reviews which
  affect the item under consideration been carried out?   dd   m   u

* Hierarchical division of system - has this item been
  broken down as required by the next design level?   d   dd   m

* Design specifications - do they adequately represent

the requirement at this level, and do they satisfy
the requirement at the previous level?   d   dd   m   u

* Interfaces - are all interfaces between software
  items fully defined?   dd   m   u

* Testing strategy and plans - do the plans represent
  an orderly and logical approach to the testing of the
  software?   d

* Development tools - have the development tools to be
  used been identified and approved?   m   u

* Maintainability - is the design structured so as to
  facilitate future maintenance?   d   dd   m   u

* Testability - will the design enable testing to be
  performed in an effective and efficient manner?   d   dd   m   u

* Test specification - have the test specifications
  been produced, and approved?   d   dd

* Test and support software - is the required test and
  support software available, and has it been approved?   d   m   u

* Documentation - have the documentation requirements
  been defined for this level, and have the documents
  been produced?   d   dd   m   u

* Design changes - what are the implications for design
  changes with regard to previously established base-
  lines?   dd   m   u

* Approval - can this level of design be approved in
  its entirety, or subject to certain restrictions?   d   dd   m   u

* Configuration management - what items, if any, must
  be placed under configuration control following the
  decisions of this review?   d   dd   m   u

* Records - have all the decisions and actions from the
  review meeting been recorded?   d   dd   m

6.4 Quality Control, Quality Assurance

6.4.1 DEFINITIONS

What we have been dealing with so far, under a variety of names, is the
quality of software. To attempt to define 'quality' is to open a major
debate - it's a bit like trying to define 'elbow grease': impossible, but

the finished article always demonstrates a lack of its presence. Let us simply say, therefore, that even though we may not be able to point to something and say "that is software quality," the lack of it is always painfully obvious.

As to the delineation of responsibility for software quality, that is more clear-cut:

"Everyone associated with a project has responsibility for the quality of software. Quality can only be achieved by building it in from inception; it cannot be added at a later stage" (EEA(1983))

From this we see that the development team carries the responsibility for the quality of the software they develop. It must be 'built-in', by virtue of the team's application of working rules - the quality controls:

"Quality Controls are the responsibility of each member of the design and development team, and are normally expressed as the controls contained in Software Standards and Engineering Codes of Practice" (EEA(1983))

Now in much the same way, a group of bus drivers might agree to control the quality of their driving by conforming to Route Standards and Highway Codes of Practice; however, the actual verification of the fact that they are doing so is not the responsibility of the driver, but of an Inspector (Bus or Police respectively):

"The verification that these rules are being applied, and applied correctly, is the purview of Quality Assurance."

"Software Quality Assurance is the responsibility of assessing whether the Standards and Codes of Practice are suitable for the job, whether they are applied in an effective and efficient manner, and whether the individual responsibilities devolved to team members within the project team are exercised." (EEA(1983))

These definitions, viewed superficially, can make quality assurance seem like some computing equivalent of the Sword of Damocles waiting to drop from its thread at the first sign of turbulence - usually on the head of the development team (or so the development team would argue). This is unfortunate since quality assurance, properly conducted, is actually an aid to all parties concerned. Different benefits accrue depending on the various perspectives. In general terms three are identified (Dunn(1982)):

Management

By providing an objective evaluation of a project's status, quality assurance enables managers to manage (and developers to develop). If this is not done then it is likely that, at the earliest, the first sign that a project is in trouble will occur at some point after testing has commenced - hardly consistent with a policy of "get it right first time"

User

Those who maintain and develop computer programs are seldom their user. As a consequence it is software quality assurance which is in the position of ensuring that what the customer receives is as complete and error-free as possible; that it can be maintained easily if an error does come to light; and that any future products reflect customer experience.

Developer

The essentials of software quality assurance are to prevent problems from occurring, remove defects, contribute to the usability and maintainability of the software - all of which amount to improving the production rate of deliverable code. Perhaps all of these might be summarised by one word: standards. By enforcing the adherence to standards, quality assurance is actually acting as the developer's friend.

Given these arguments, the more enlightened software developers will carry out their own quality assurance activity. Major customers, such as MOD, will expect their own quality assurance personnel to assume responsibility in this area. Either way the outcome should be 'quality' software if the job is done well - which is justification enough.

6.4.2 ASPECTS OF SOFTWARE QUALITY ASSURANCE

The major software quality assurance activities during the project life-cycle are summarised below: we note in passing, however, that the list could be extended by considering the benefits of having quality assurance activity begin before development actually gets under way - just as the police might be consulted with some profit before an illegal design for an articulated treble-decker bus goes into mass production!

* Take an active part in design reviews;

* ensure that all aspects of the design and development are documented in sufficient detail to provide an historic record for design review and post design purposes;

* review the test and acceptance plans to ensure that they adequately demonstrate all the features of the requirement specification;

* review the software test procedures to ensure that they constitute both a reasonable and realistic test of all the features of the software;

* monitor, by appropriate audits, the various software activities and to confirm that the defined software standards are adhered to;

* participate in testing and the associated analysis of results;

* approve and record the configuration of the software on which the development and testing was carried out;

* review the organisation's quality assurance activities relating to software.

6.5 Planning to Test

The foregoing should have indicated that management and planning are both essential components of a successful software development programme; that they should be regarded, in the broadest sense, as elements of the design process for the project as whole. Reviews, configuration control, quality controls and assurance - each has as its objective the prevention of errors at the earliest possible stage. A romantic might suggest that together they march under the banner of "get it right first time".

For precisely the same reason a well-planned project will look forward to the day when an implemented version of the design is ready to be tested. It will aim to maximise the effectiveness of discovering errors by early and controlled production of Test Plans and Test Specifications.

A Test Plan is essentially a strategy document. It defines, for the software product as a whole, the testing philosophy, the stages and sequence of tests, and the procedures to be followed. It will be complemented by a series of Test Specifications, which provide the detail for a particular test or series of tests.

Hopefully the value of doing this sort of thing is self-evident. If not, here is another reason. At the outset, everybody concerned with the project expects the testing to take place within the agreed timescales. But when the project falls behind schedule pressures, and/or temptations, grow to cut short the testing phases so as to meet the deadline. The existence of agreed test plans and specifications serves to act as a curb to that happening. On the other hand, if it does happen then they at least provide a summary of what has been skimped.

6.5.1 TEST PLAN

The Test Plan would be produced as early as possible in the project life-cycle, and be updated whenever necessary in response to changes elsewhere in the development programme. It should address the following areas:

6.5.1.1 Test Philosophy

A rather esoteric title, perhaps best illustrated by a simple example.

"Nice design, Arthur. A flying four-door family saloon could be a real winner. How you gonna test it?"
"Well, the lads've all got their different bits to make .."
"Right."
"So they all make their bits, and then we join 'em all up .."
"Right?"
"Wheel it out, and see if it takes off."

In this instance, a (probably literal) 'big-bang' testing philosophy is being advocated. It may not be good, but it is a philosophy. A test philosophy, then, outlines the approach to be taken in testing the product. It should give a clear indication of the levels and degree of testing that are felt necessary.

In practice, no complex system can ever be completely tested. Eventually a point will be reached at which the law of diminishing returns applies, with the effort expended in conducting further tests being out of all proportion to the results achieved. The task is thus made manageable by reducing the complexity of what is to be tested. If the product has a well-defined structure, a hierarchy of modules being the most obvious, then it is possible for tests to be localised so as to maximise the impact they have - more little tests rather than a few giant ones in other words. A test philosophy which decrees at the outset that it requires testing to be conducted at the module, sub-module and unit levels of the detailed design thereby influences that design for the better. Chapter 9 gives some practical examples of testing based on structured design.

A further area of test philosophy deals with logistics. Arthur's mate might have suggested that the flying-car design could be more safely tested by means of a simulation system. Our multi-user telephone directory system might also employ this technique as an alternative to scouring the streets for hundreds of keyboard operators to help with the performance tests.

6.5.1.2 Test Stages and Sequences

In very broad terms, three separate test stages are implied by the project life-cycle:

*   Module testing - 'independent' testing of sections of code. Since ter-
    minolgy can become very suspect here, so let us say that what we are
    talking about is the testing of the functionality of the module - does
    it do what it is supposed to do? If the module is made up of a number
    of sub-modules and units then the same sort of test would be applied
    to each of these component sections.

*   Integration testing - the testing of two or more modules operating
    together. Here the emphasis, assuming that module testing has done its
    job, is on proving the interactions between the modules: that they
    operate correctly as an integrated whole. Depending on the complexity
    of the system, integration tests may be conducted at a range of code
    levels.

* Acceptance testing - it works, but does it work properly? Testing for
  acceptance means using the software in a real situation (or an
  acceptable simulation e.g. for nuclear power station process control)
  so as to prove that it meets the requirements specification in terms
  of both functionality and performance.

The test plan will relate these stages both to the software design and the
requirements specification so as to identify the test stages for the
project and, thereby, the objectives of the tests to be conducted at those
stages.

Sequence - the order in which the various tests are to be carried out - is
also important:

"Mark II, eh Arthur? How're you going to test this one?"
"I'm going for a structured approach. Test it bit by bit .."
"Right."
"starting with the wings .."

The plan will stipulate test sequences that are logical. Just what is logical for a particular system requires careful analysis. Much will depend
upon the ways in which the various modules interrelate with each other; a
well-planned ordering of the integration tests can both exercise a wider
range of possible events and minimise the amount of special-purpose test
software that has to be produced. The test sequence should thus be used as
the basis for a production schedule - "wings can wait .. give me an
engine first."

6.5.1.3 Procedures

General procedures for the conduct of tests are primarily concerned with:

* Test results: procedures for documenting, summarising and reviewing the
                results of tests;

* Test failure: (test success?) what to do when errors are discovered in
                the software being tested;

* Test changes: altering the agreed test specification/sequence for any
                reason.

As might be expected, these procedures will lean quite heavily on the
review processes described in 6.3; also, such is human nature, they will
be more formally invoked as testing nears acceptance stages.

6.5.2 TEST SPECIFICATIONS

A Test Specification, as its title suggests, provides details for a specific test. It will be uniquely identified and documented so as to be available for later reference. Essentially it covers the What, Why and How of testing.

* What is to be tested. This could range from the test of a coded unit, or even a section of code, to the the integration test of a number of modules, up to the final acceptance testing of the final article.

  [e.g. "to test Procedure COMPARE of module SEARCH"]

* Why it is to be tested. The objective of the test. Again the range is wide, from the proving of a particular algorithm through to the verification of a performance limitation. Whatever the case, the objective should relate to the appropriate part of the requirements specification.

  [e.g. "to verify the comparison algorithm of COMPARE for a range of names and telephone number combinations. The comparison forms part of the requirement to Search for and/or Modify a stored record"]

* How it is to be tested. A section made up of a number of parts:

  Test data: items of data being used in the test;
  Test results: expected results using this data;
  Test records: how the results and findings are being recorded;
  Configuration: details of software elements linked to the item under
      test.

6.6 Summary

* Verification and testing do not happen by chance: they are planned and managed.

* As software is developed its parts - configuration items - change many times; configuration management is required to control these changes and relate them to defined baselines.

* Configuration management of code is a special problem.

* Design reviews, through formal inspection and approval of designs, play a major role in verification at all design levels.

* Quality controls are the responsibility of the project team; quality assurance, in verifying that quality control rules are being obeyed, actually serves all concerned.

* Test plans and specifications are drawn up the same time as designs, and are subject to the same process of review.

6.7 Things to Think About

*   Identify configuration items and baselines for a bicycle, Arthur's caroplane or Frankenstein's monster and produce an outline design.

*   Do the same for a word processing package.

*   Prepare check-lists for a design review on one of the above, for each of: management, customer, programmer.

*   Devise a test plan for one of your designs.

*   At what point should quality assurance become involved in a project?

CHAPTER SEVEN

Programming Languages

"To God I speak Spanish, to women Italian,
to men French, and to my horse - German."

Attr. to Emperor Charles V

7.1   Choice of Programming Language

When it comes to turning a design into a program, Charles provides a model
for all software engineers: choose the language to suit the application. A
language which is ideal for the implementation of a business system could
well be the most awful language in which to develop a scientific package;
real-time process control systems are different from real-time commercial
systems, and the same programming language may not be applicable to both.

As we have seen in chapters 4 and 5 the design specifications, although
language-independent, will necessarily influence the choice of language
both by their assumption that the design is indeed capable of realisation
in whatever programming language is used and, to a lesser extent, by the
design methodology employed. The influence, though, is more to do with the
structures and facilities offered by the language in general rather than
language specifics; given a free choice from any of the many hundreds of
programming languages in existence quite a few could be found to fit the
bill.

Which is where the theory bumps up against the realities of practice. To
all intents and purposes a free choice of programming language is never
available. At best there might be a free choice from a few languages; at
worst, the language will have been determined before design has even
started. Some of the reasons for this situation are as follows:

* A translator for the chosen programming language may not be available for the hardware configuration to be used. If it exists, it will have to be acquired. Translators - themselves complex software items - are expensive, and the cost of purchasing one for the ideal language will have to be offset against the savings made by using a less-than-ideal language for which a translator has already been bought for another project. If an implementation of the translator doesn't exist for the hardware configuration in question, then the costs will be even higher of course.

* Unlike the Emperor, existing programming staff may not be fluent in a wide range of languages, including the ideal language. This is not an insurmountable problem of course, but could have a bearing on the decision.

* Previous projects have been written in a different language. Apart from the fact that experience will have been gained in the use of this other language, this may be a telling factor if the previous projects are in any way related to the project under discussion. (This argument is, of course, self-perpetuating for the language that is chosen).

* The user may stipulate that a particular programming language is to be used, or chosen from a short list - suitable or not. For instance, the the Ministry of Defence now stipulate in their contracts that ADA must be the language used (previously the requirement was CORAL 66). Unless the supplier can persuade the customer to accept an alternative then a choice just does not exist at all. If the customer is going to take on program maintenance at some future time, then the reasoning behind this constraint actually boils down to those given above regarding previous projects and programming staff.

* No ideal language exists! If this is the case then the alternatives are to invest the time and money in designing a new, ideal, language and writing a translator for it or to make the most of a language that is less-than-ideal. The former choice can be practical for very large projects: the language C aided and abetted the development of the UNIX operating system, for instance.

Even when impracticable, it would seem that implementing a new programming language is a route that is often taken - which explains why there is a veritable computing Tower of Babel to choose from when this is allowed.

In practice, however, the choice will inevitably come down to one of only a small number of programming languages which have gained sufficient standing to be in widespread use. But what makes a programming language popular? And why, with so many languages in existence, are new ones still being designed? To get some idea of the answers to these questions, and their relevance to software engineering, there follows a potted history of programming language evolution through a discussion of what Pressman(1982) calls the 'foundation languages': FORTRAN, COBOL, BASIC and ALGOL.

7.2 A History of Programming Languages

7.2.1 FORTRAN

Much as the act of standing on two legs instead of all fours marked the
moment at which man moved ahead of the rest of the animal kingdom, so the
arrival of FORTRAN in 1962 signalled the supremacy of the high-level language over assembly languages. The latter, basically one-to-one representations of the instruction sets and addressing mechanisms of computer
architectures, confined the programmer in a strait-jacket of detail, with
such things as simple arithmetic expressions having to be coded in terms
of individual computational steps. FORTRAN, in allowing the programmer to
use something like natural arithmetic notation for program steps, became
an immediate star simply because it was the first in the sky.

Since that time the language has been fiercely criticised for its lack of
structure, weak data typing and general incomprehensibilty - but is still
the most widely-used language for scientific and engineering applications.
The reasons for this are salutary.

Firstly the language has changed, has evolved, with FORTRAN 77 being the
currently accepted standard. Like the broom which has a new head one year,
and a new handle the next, it may still be called by the same name, but it
is very different from the original.

Secondly, for all its deficiencies, FORTRAN users were reluctant to part
company with the language because of their investment in it. Continued use
over the early years when the language stood alone meant that when alternative languages did arrive on the scene users were actually unable to
move from FORTRAN because of the need to convert their existing programs
if they did. By moving with later versions of the language this trauma was
avoided.

The implications of the FORTRAN story for software engineers are profound:
the choice of language, if a choice is available, must be made with the
utmost care since it may well influence future development for a long time
thereafter.

7.2.2 COBOL

In some ways the COBOL story parallels that of FORTRAN. Developed at about
the same time COBOL is still the accepted programming language for large-
scale commercial data processing application areas such as insurance and
banking. Its aims (Higman(1977)) were to:

* attempt to be a subset of English, and thereby readable (although
  not writeable) by the uninitiated;

* cater for data structures of the sort found in typical office records;

* aim at a realistic means of attaining complete compatibility.

Whilst the first objective failed dismally - many opponents arguing that COBOL was hard to read, let alone write, even by the initiated - the other aims were notably successful. COBOL's approach to data and code separation has to be given credit for its worth in software engineering terms, and the value of seeking to define a standard implementation for the language across a range of host machines accepted, if not followed, by all who see the cost benefits of program portability.

Like FORTRAN, COBOL has a developed over the years and, with its enormous user base, has not been supplanted by other languages - such as PL/1 - which were fully expected to take its place.

7.2.3 BASIC

The arrival of BASIC in 1965 was significant, not so much because of the features offered by the language, but because of the fact that it was designed to be used interactively rather than via a Batch system. BASIC was also a ridiculously easy language to learn (an essential - it was designed for computer science students). Views differ; depending on who you talk to the easiness and interactiveness of BASIC are either its main advantages or its biggest disadvantages. Certainly the language has undergone a quite remarkable revival through the medium of the microcomputer, and its very existence must have encouraged many to persevere with computing in a way that an initial exposure to a more complicated programming language. All those people with bad habits ..

In software engineering terms BASIC, as a language, has a large number of deficiencies, many of which have been pointed out in this book. But as a program development system, incorporating such things as an editor, and a trace facility, BASIC undoubtedly promoted the moves towards integrated programming support.

7.2.4 ALGOL

It is ironic that, alone out of the four foundation languages, the name ALGOL should have disappeared from current terminology since, although never really adopted in any large measure by the commercial world, ALGOL's influence on programming language design has been enormous. In its original form ALGOL-60 ("a great improvement on most of its successors", said C.A.R.Hoare) was the first language to have a formally-defined syntax and associated semantics (ALGOL(1962)). It incorporated block structures, data typing, and local variable declarations - all seen today as essentials for a programming language for software engineering.

Although the name died after a later version, ALGOL-68, failed to live up to expectations, the spirit of the language lives on - chiefly in Pascal (Jensen(1975)). Many of the Pascal features promoted in this book as being highly desirable in a programming language had their origins in ALGOL.

In its turn, Pascal has been the progenitor of other languages. Modula-2 shares its father (Wirth) with Pascal, and ADA - recently developed under the direction of the U.S. Department of Defense as their language for the future - admits to having been strongly influenced by Pascal.

The common feature of all these languages is structure: each of them lends itself to the writing of programs which flow directly from the types of sound design methodology that have been discussed in earlier sections.

7.2.5 THE REST

The foundation languages were designed to meet particular needs: FORTRAN and ALGOL for scientific applications, COBOL for business, and BASIC as a teaching tool. Of the many languages to have followed them, only a few aimed at becoming a sort of computing Esperanto, satisfying a wide range of applications, and none have met with universal acclaim. Only PL/1 has made a significant mark, but even this is due more to its association with IBM systems than any intrinsic merit. ADA is the newest 'all-singing, all-dancing' language, and it will be interesting to see how widely used it will be in the future with non-defence projects.

Specialised languages form by far the majority of the remainder. In every case the argument for expending the development effort is that the application area demands a language with a particular vocabulary and structure. Systems development (BCPL, C), string handling (SNOBOL), report generation (RPG), simulation (SIMULA) list processing and artificial intelligence (LISP and PROLOG) - all have had new languages designed in their cause. If - or rather, when - further programming languages arrive on the scene, they will almost certainly be specialised languages.

For the software engineer, the guiding principles in evaluating newcomers will be those that we have tried to illustrate in this book: how well does the language form any integral and coherent part of the whole process of design and implementation?

7.3 Program Implementation in Basic and Pascal

Chapters 4 and 5 sought to answer this question for BASIC an Pascal at the design level. We now look at some of the features of these two languages in the light of some implementation requirements; in particular, defensive programming and systems performance.

Defensive programming is equivalent to performing your own medical examination. By regularly measuring your pulse-rate, taking your temperature and inspecting different parts of your anatomy for unexpected lumps and bumps, the likelihood of your suddenly collapsing in a heap is diminished. In the same way, by using programming language facilities, a program can detect operational faults before they turn into something serious.

Systems performance - for instance, the ability of the system to meet certain requirements in terms of timing or memory occupancy - will also be an implementation issue that can be influenced by the way in which the software is written. In the same way that an athlete, required to run a four-minute mile, is not going to wear wellington boots so a programmer should be able to pick the tools for the job.

7.3.1 DATA INITIALISATION

On some computer configurations the first appearance of a data object can be assumed to have an initial value. This is typically the case with BASIC, where many implementations set real and integer variables to zero on the commencement of program execution. Defensive programming would not use this rather misguided 'facility' but explicitly initialise the content of all such variables as part of the program code. Unless this is done the program could fail in a random fashion - on re-entry to the code with the variable non-zero, for instance.

Common examples of the need for data initialisation are the use of integer variables as counters, and boolean variables as flags, e.g.

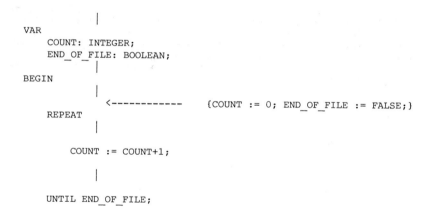

```
         |
VAR
     COUNT: INTEGER;
     END_OF_FILE: BOOLEAN;
         |
BEGIN
         |
              <------------      {COUNT := 0; END_OF_FILE := FALSE;}
     REPEAT
         |

     COUNT := COUNT+1;

         |

     UNTIL END_OF_FILE;
```

Ideally, not the case in either BASIC or Pascal, such initialisation of variables would be forced by the programming language itself.

The same problem applies to the initial setting of values for larger data structures such as arrays. Here, the action will often involve the reading of data from a file - a process difficult to check visually. For once, a facility in BASIC is quite handy in this respect. The READ statement, although called an input command, actually takes values specified within the program as DATA, and assigns them to variables.

```
e.g.    10   DIM NAMES$(6)
        20   FOR I% = 1 TO 6
        30   READ NAME$(I%)
        40   NEXT I%

             |


      1000   DATA JAKE, JENNIFER, STEPHEN, CATHERINE, ANOTHER1, ANOTHER2
```

Not perfect, but visibility is increased.

7.3.2 CONSTANTS

Constants are data objects which do not change their value during the execution of a program. In terms of defensive programming their use is recommended for two reasons:

In Pascal, an attempt to change the value of a CONST item will be detected and produce an error at run-time. For this reason, as was outlined in chapter 4, constant values should be identified by data analysis and built into the program code.

Another reason for doing this, however, is that it lessens the chances of error if, for any reason, that constant is changed by design - necessitating alteration to every point in the program at which the value is used. Consider, for instance, a document production program which has to keep a value for the number of lines on a page:

```
e.g.            |

        CONST
            Page_length = 60;

        BEGIN
               |
            No_of_chars := Page_length * Line_length
               |
            IF Lines_printed = Page_length THEN .....
               |
        END.
```

Changing Page_length to any other value means an alteration to one program line only. If the actual value is inserted in the text of the program rather than the identifier (i.e. 60 as opposed to page_length), then the whole text has to be scanned so that all the appropriate alterations can been made - with the danger that one will be missed.

BASIC does not have any mechanism by which constants may be distinguished from variables. From the examples cited above the page length would have to be assigned to a variable. The major problem here is that there is no assurance that the constant value remains unaltered. Since it is a variable it may appear on the left hand side of an assignment statement. Whether such an action is deliberate or accidental is irrelevant; since it is a possibility the whole program has to be checked. A software engineer's nightmare.

7.3.3 TYPES OF VARIABLES

Choose the variable to do the job. As far as arithmetic operations are concerned, never use a real where an integer will do.

Those who have grown up with BASIC, in which real variables are assumed by default, may have a mental block about the need for integers at all. Quite simply, an integer representation of a value is exact, whereas a real is only an approximation. Blanket use of real variables, therefore, will at some stage involve a comparison of two reals which may work in theory (and be supported by run-time output) but fail in practice. At its extreme this can include the failure of something like a FOR statement in which the control variable is a real.

Defensive programming by use of integer variables, or by effecting real comparisons by including a tolerance factor,

    e.g   IF X1 - X2 < 0.00001 THEN .....

will avoid such situations.

In terms of performance, use of integer variables (and boolean variables, which amount to the same thing) will increase processing speeds: execution times can be reduced by up to 50% over the use of real variables, simply because computers take longer to perform real calculations than integer ones.

7.3.4 SUBRANGES

Every data value will have a range of permitted values; that range may be infinite, but it exists. The use of subranges in a language such as Pascal is defensive programming made easy. By declaring in a subrange the expected values for a variable, an automatic checking mechanism will be invoked: for example, given the Pascal declaration:

```
        CONST
            Age_limit = 100;
            Sample_space = 10;

        TYPE
            Letter : 'a' .. 'z';
            Digit : '0' .. '9';

        VAR
            My_age : 1 .. Age_limit;
            Alpha : Letter;
            Beta : Digit;
            Sample : -Sample_space .. Sample_space;
```

the following examples of incorrect assignments would be detected during
compilation:

```
            Alpha := '7';
            Beta := 'f';
            Sample := 16;
```

Furthermore, the following would produce a run-time error if the value of
variable My_age was greater than 1:

```
            Sample := My_age * 10 ;
```

There is no equivalent mechanism in BASIC. This means that every variable
is legitimately able to take the maximum value for its type. To attempt
defensive programming for every possible instance of a value going out of
range is totally impracticable.

Note, however, that there is a price to pay in terms of performance - you
get nothing for nothing. Subrange checking is carried out out run-time by
additional system code which has to be executed, and that inevitably adds
to the execution time. Lose the overhead - which is usually an option -
and you lose the facility.

7.3.5 ARRAY HANDLING

A similar technique can be employed with arrays, since the dimension of
an array is effectively a subrange itself (of the index used to access the
array):

```
    e.g.   CONST
            Character_length = 5;   {Length of character string}

        TYPE
            Index : 1 .. Character_length;
            String_length : 1 .. Character_length;
            String : PACKED ARRAY [ String_length ] OF CHAR;
```

Array bound checking is quite regularly conducted by run-time systems of virtually every language. Even BASIC does it! What happens, however, is that the error is detected at the point at which an attempt is made to access the array with a subscript which does not conform with the array dimension; trying to use array element String [Index], where Index has a value of 6 is equivalent to referencing a non-existent variable.

What the programmer wants to know, however, is where Index got its value 6 from. Often the assignment is in the vicinity of the array reference (a FOR loop, for instance) but it can be some way off - especially if the index is being passed as a parameter to a procedure responsible for manipulating the array. Use of a subrange for both the index and the array bound will cover all eventualities.

Once again, these checks will have an adverse affect on run times.

7.3.6 DATA INPUT

All input data should be checked for validity before being passed on to the rest of the program for processing. Although much of this checking can be carried out by the use of subrange facilities if they exist, there will necessarily exist a number of other things that can wrong.

As an example, the first input that many programs require is the current date - perhaps input as 3 integer values representing day, month and year. Now each of these values can have an associated subrange:

```
VAR
    Day : 1 .. 31;
    Month : 1 .. 12;
    Year : 1 .. 2000; {say}
```

But subrange checking alone is insufficient in this case because the validity of the date is linked to combinations of the three variables, not individual instances of their value. Thus a value of 31 for day is fine if month is 3, but not if month is 4. Validity checking in this case means a not insignificant amount of specially-written defensive code:

```
VAR
    Leap_year: BOOLEAN;
    Daysin : ARRAY [1 .. 12] OF INTEGER;

            |

BEGIN

    Daysin [4] := 30; Daysin [5] := 31; Daysin [6] := [30];
    Daysin [7] := 31; Daysin [8] := 31; Daysin [9] := [30];
    Daysin [10] := 31; Daysin [11] := 30; Daysin [12] := [31];

    {input Day, Month and Year - with subrange checking}
```

```
        Leap_year := Day MOD 4 = 0; {should really be more complex}

   IF Day > Daysin [Month]
        THEN proc_error
        ELSE IF NOT (Leap_year AND Day=29 AND Month=2)
             THEN proc_error;


        {date valid}

                        |

        END.
```

All rather unpleasant, but very necessary. It is possible that for complex
data entry the program statements for validation can quite easily amount
to a significant proportion of the overall code.

Another problem associated with data input is the loss of data: that is,
data values which not actually reaching the program at all. This fault is
readily apparent if the program is being run interactively, because one
gets to feel like Canute in trying to hold back the waves of input prompt
messages that keep on coming. If input is being taken from backing
store, however, a series of values may end up with the wrong variables
- leading either to errors because of type clashes or, at worst, incorrect
results being generated. This sort of thing is a regular occurrence where
Pascal READLN statements are being incorrectly used instead of READ and
values at the end of a line being dropped.

Defensive programming requires not only that input values should be valid,
but seen to be valid: when in doubt, print it out. Of course a thorough
software engineer is always in doubt.

7.3.7 EXCEPTION HANDLING

A major problem area is that of the system error - a fault condition that
is detected either by the computer operating system, or the language run-
time routines. In cases like this only two choices are open to the software engineer. The first is to accept that the program will be regarded by
the operating system as being beyond help, and summarily abandoned with an
error message likely to mean very little to the user. The second, which is
much more effort, is to include within the program what is termed an
exception handling routine which will take command of the situation and
try to recover from it. Unfortunately, even if the second course is
followed (which, ideally, it should be) the programming language is likely
to be found wanting.

Let us illustrate the magnitude of the problem with a simple, but typical,
example. A database program has a menu option which allows records to be
added to a file. Within the program this is achieved by a small hierarchy
of two procedures which input the record and write it to disc respect-

ively, together with the main program which controls the menu responses. The exception that has to be guarded against is that of the database becoming full. In Pascal, an outline solution would be as follows:

```
            |
VAR
     Database_full : BOOLEAN

PROCEDURE Input_rec ...
BEGIN
            |
     IF NOT Database_full
       THEN Write_rec ...
       ELSE Handle_error
            |
END;

PROCEDURE Write_rec ...
BEGIN
            |
     IF NOT Database_full
       THEN { send record to disc }
       ELSE Handle_error;

     Database_full := {system variable for end_of_file}
            |
END;

PROCEDURE Handle_error ...
BEGIN
            |
END;

{main program starts here}
BEGIN
     Database_full := FALSE;
            |
     CASE menu-choice OF
            |
         ADD: IF NOT Database_full
                THEN Input_rec ...
                ELSE Handle_error
            |
     END;
            |
END.
```

Other solutions to this problem are equally messy in Pascal. Because the language lacks any specific structures for exception handling, the only ways open are like that shown: using a global variable and conducting tests for the database being full at each level of the hierarchy. Although unpleasant, it only in this way can we be sure that the operating system will not be asked to write to a full database file and cause a system break.

As it happens, BBC BASIC is more helpful in this respect. It has a variant
of the ON statement, ON ERROR, which can be used to switch error handling
from the operating system to a nominated section of the BASIC program. For
instance,

```
10    ON ERROR PROC_ERR


1000  DEF PROC_ERR
1010  IF ERR = 223 THEN ... : ENDPROC
1020  PRINT "ERROR "; ERR;" IN LINE ";ERL': REPORT
1030  ENDPROC
```

would cause PROC_ERR to be entered when any error condition was detected.
By checking for the particular system error number (223) for end-of-file,
specific exception action could be taken. Note, however, that it is a case
of all or nothing with this facility: every error has to be handled by the
routine, even if its action, as above, is to do no more than to mimic the
system and output an error number.

Exception handling is worth a chapter on its own. Even if a routine has
been written, and can be entered automatically, what happens after the
routine has been executed? Is it possible to recover the situation and
continue with the program run - and, if so, at what point? Even a 'clean'
solution such as returning to the menu presentation part of the main program is likely to leave an untidy position behind in terms of incomplete
procedure calls. Sommerville(1985) raises the questions that need to be
borne in mind when assessing programming language design in this area:

*   How should exceptions be declared?

*   Where should exception handlers be placed in a program?

*   Should exception handlers be a distinct program structure, or should
    exceptions be handled using existing structures such as procedures?

*   How should exceptions be signalled and transmitted from one program
    unit to another?

*   Should exceptions and exception handlers be subject to the normal
    scope and extent rules of the language?

*   Should exception handlers cause control to be returned to the point
    where the exception occurred after it has been dealt with?

Developments in the language ADA appear to have made significant strides
in the direction of adequate structures for exception handling; the reader
is referred to Barnes(1984), or any of the other texts on ADA, for further
information.

7.4 The Use of Assembly Language

For the sake of completeness, we consider briefly the place of assembly language in the software engineer's armoury. Some might express the view that it has no place at all. Assembly languages take much longer to write and debug; they do not lend themselves to structured programming; they disguise design detail so completely that it is virtually impossible to identify the context for any group of program statements; by virtue of their close relationship with the machine architecture, they open up new vistas for wierd and wonderful programming errors.

And yet, with all their disadvantages, assembly languages are still doing their bit in the world of software development, particularly in the implementation of embedded systems. In part this is due to such systems needing to be based on microprocessors for which no high-level language has been developed; it can only be hoped that this situation will change quickly, especially as ADA gains ground.

Aside from this particular area, assembly language retains a foothold for - supposedly - two reasons: programs written in assembler require less memory, and run faster. Whether these factors are sufficiently critical for a project to dispense with high-level language development, either in all or in part, can often be insufficiently considered.

As regards memory, a high-level language compiler will generate code which requires more memory than that of an equivalent assembly language program. But, for one thing, many systems require the majority of their memory for data not code and so the actual excess may be a small proportion of the overall requirement. For another, with the price of memory coming down and the capacity of individual chips rocketing up, the amount of memory needed is ceasing to be an important factor.

Execution speed is a different matter. A compiler will inevitably produce machine code that lacks the efficiency of software hand-coded by a good assembly language programmer. In situations which require software to run under severe time constraints, the assembly language solution may be the only way of reaching the target. However, this is not to say that a whole program has to be coded in assembler. If it can be determined which parts of the program are critical (and it can - see Profiling in chapter 9) then only those parts will need to be recoded, with the remainder left in high-level language. The feasibility of this as a solution will depend on what software development tools are available - chapter 8 is about to describe what is necessary.

7.5 Summary

* Whilst in theory the programmer can choose from a wide range of programming languages, in practice the choice is very restricted.

* Four foundation languages have had a major influence on programming

language design. Of these ALGOL-60 and its successors - particularly Pascal and ADA - are the languages best suited to structured software development.

* Defensive programming and systems performance are prime considerations when a program is design is implemented; software engineers should be aware of whatever facilities their programming language may have in this respect.

* The particular problem of exception handling may only be capable of solution through non-structured programming.

* Assembly language should only be used as a last resort, and in minimal amounts, to boost execution speed.

7.6 Things to Think About

* What would be the implications of an organisation with a wide range of existing packages in FORTRAN or BASIC electing to have all their future software products developed in Pascal?

* Why did Latin die and FORTRAN survive?

* How does menu-driven software assist in the requirement for defensive programming?

* What are the difficulties in using the ON ERROR mechanism as provided by BBC BASIC for exception handling? What happens if the error routine has an error in it?

* Implement a CASE statement in assembly language, and judge it for such things as structure and visibility of design.

CHAPTER EIGHT

Software Development: Techniques and Tools

"Responsible for this work of development were 'the boys
in the back rooms' who 'do not sit in the limelight but
are the men who do the work'"

(report of broadcast by) Lord Beaverbrook,
Glasgow Herald, March 1941

8.1   Introduction

The word 'engineer' as used in the term 'software engineer' should suggest
two things. Firstly, as we have been at pains to point out time and again,
it suggests that a person so titled will always approach the task of software production in a controlled and professional manner, employing well-
defined techniques.

The second is an implied suggestion: that the software engineer will be
adept in the use of software engineering tools. A suitable analogy is that
of a mechanical engineer when producing, for example, an engine component
from specifications supplied through technical drawings and other job
specification documents. In producing the component the mechanical engineer will have a whole range of tools at his/her disposal, and the
efficiency with which the job is completed will depend on the suitability
of those tools and their effective use by the engineer.

Although the adage ' a poor craftsman always blames his tools ' is valid
under certain conditions it is difficult to see how engineers can be
expected to perform their duties efficiently and effectively without the
necessary equipment. A qualitative and quantative assessment of a software
engineer, then, should not be solely based upon whether the produced
software satisfactorily achieves what is requested within predefined
timescales - consideration should also be given to the support tools

available. Conversely, consideration should be given to what support tools are going to be required before project timescales are fixed.

Before considering a basic tool-kit, a word about the environment within which they will be used. Nowadays it is virtually certain that the mode of operation will be interactive, via a keyboard and a monitor. This is fine: armed with the most basic facilities it is possible for the software engineer tobe highly effective when working interactively. It is also quite possible for an interactive facility to be horribly abused, by using its convenience as a substitute for forethought and planning (students seem to adopt this mode of working as though to the manner born). Unless the use of the available tools is allied to a controlled development strategy any benefit achieved will be purely coincidental.

A basic set of software engineering tools would be those needed for:

a) the preparation of an item of program source code;

b) the translation of this code into a machine-level form;

c) the linking of the machine-code with other, similar, items to form a program that can be executed;

d) the verification of its run-time performance;

e) the amendment of the original source program so as to remove errors;

Item d) is covered separately in chapter 9 on testing and debugging. Item a) is actually a subset of e), since the latter will necessarily include the capability to prepare source code. Both are thus considered in the next section on program editing, followed by b) - program translation - and c) - program building.

8.2 Program Editing

On the reasonable assumption that the source program is to be held in a disc file - whether it is to be subsequently run interactively or under a batch processing system - there are requirements to create that file in the first place and, subsequently, to alter its contents. The tool used for this purpose is called an Editor and, almost without exception, it will be a tool used interactively. There are basically two types of editors: Line Editors and Screen Editors.

A line editor is something of an anachronism, its general design dating back to the 'teletype' days when paper was provided instead of a screen. Conceptually, therefore, the user of a line editor works through his file on a line-by-line basis, the line available for alteration at any moment being termed the 'current line'. The current line is moved by means of a command, e.g. move on 5 lines. Only this line is displayed (on request, usually!), with a list command having to be used in order to determine the whereabouts of the line in the file. A current listing is almost essential to have at hand, therefore.

Screen editors present a full screen of text at a time. The user moves
the cursor around the screen - normally by use of a set of special keys on
the keyboard - to locate the position of the modification to be made.
The unit of the file available for editing is therefore equivalent to the
capacity of the screen. It may also be possible to scroll backwards and
forwards through the file, effectively providing a larger unit than the
screen capacity.

Basic locate operations apart, both types of editor will provide similar,
'long-distance' locative commands to find, for instance 'the first line
containing the character string xyz'. Likewise, the actual edit operations
will be similar in function, but with the Screen Editor allowing the user
to see the changes take place on the screen. Generally speaking the
individual facilities provided by both include the ability to insert and
delete and replace - with either whole lines or parts of a line - perform
multiple edits on a line or throughout a file, and so on.

The fancier the facilities the more careful the user has to be to handle
them correctly. For example the ability to globally edit every occurrence
of the character string ' X_coord : INTEGER ' by its replacement ' X_coord
: REAL ' is very useful. However there may be occurrences of ' X_coord :
INTEGER ' which are declared locally within sub-programs which should
remain unaffected. Unless one can guarantee that the effect of such a
global edit is assured then it shouldn't be used. This is particularly
true in cases where not all of the source text is known to the user; it
is perfectly possible to finish an edit session with a file containing
more errors than it started with.

BASIC, of course, has its own built-in editing system: to modify a line in
the source program, type it in again with the same line number as before.
In addition, most systems will offer some sort of machine-related facility
involving special keys on the keyboard; BBC BASIC, for instance, accords a
special meaning to a COPY key to enable sections of a previously typed
line to be duplicated for re-input. These are not file editors, however,
just ways in which a BASIC program can be read in, changed, and written
out to disc again.

Pascal has no equivalent mode of operation. A Pascal program will be held
in a file, and an Editor invoked by a special command stipulating the file
to be operated upon. Either type of editor is adequate, although a screen
editor is obviously preferable; the UCSD Pascal system as described by
Bowles (1980) is a popular microcomputer implementation in this respect.

8.3   Program Translation

Before a program can be run on a computer it has to be translated into a
form suitable for execution. Although something of an over-simplification,
two broad approaches can be taken to the task of translation. The source
code can be interpreted (as is normal with BASIC), the execution effect-

ively being based on the source code itself, with no other version of the program being generated. Alternatively it can be compiled (as with Pascal), so as to produce another, machine-level, version of the program capable of execution.

The generic names for the tools used in these modes of translation are the Interpreter and the Compiler respectively.

8.3.1 INTERPRETERS

An interpreter performs the translation of the source text into a 'machine code', and effects the execution of that code, in one go. Thus, when a BASIC program has been input, the command RUN causes the BASIC interpreter to both translate and execute each statement it meets in the sequence of the program flow of control. This happens for every statement, whether or not that statement has been met before; thus statements within a FOR-loop construct will be retranslated every time round the loop. As a result of this somewhat laborious process the execution time of a program is considerably longer than if it were already compiled.

Associated with this mode of operation is the fact that the whole of the source program needs to reside in memory, along with the interpreter, throughout the execution of the program. This obviusly affects the size of the programs that can be run.

On the credit side, however, because interpretive systems are interactive by defintion, when a run-time (which may be syntactical, of course) error is detected the program stops and reports the fact immediately. Because the source program is available, it is possible to give a positive indication as to the type and location of the error. Together with the easy availability of an integrated source code Editor, an interpretive system can undoubtedly make software development that much easier and quicker.

8.3.2 COMPILERS

8.3.2.1 Principles of Compilation

When a source text is submitted to a compiler it undergoes a total trans-formation as a single entity: all instructions are converted into their respective machine executable statements, all symbolic names are trans-lated into machine addresses with enough memory space being allocated to store the specified data values, all data constants are stored in areas from which they may easily be retrieved. By considering all of the text in one go the compiler is able to resolve many syntactical errors at a time by considering more complex issues such as scope of variables and illegal accesses, inappropriate nesting of loops and subprograms, incomplete control constructs, etc.

A compiler effectively carries out its task in four stages:

* Lexical analysis: converts the external form into a more concise form for internal storage, removing such things as redundant spaces;

* Syntax analysis: checking of statements for 'grammatical' errors: it is at this stage that error messages are produced;

* Optimisation: (which could be more-or-less absent) scanning the valid source code for commonality, so that duplicate code is not produced unnecesarily;

* Code generation: the production of an 'object' form of the program.

An effective syntax analysis stage is important for the software engineer. When an error is detected by the compiler it will be logged in a listing (or some temporary) file. The compilation will continue either until the end of the source text is reached, or the compiler has encountered so many errors that it is totally confused and throws in the towel. The helpfulness of the error messages is all-important: they should atempt to do two things: give an indication as to the type of error detected, and an indication of its whereabouts - chapter 9, on debugging, gives some examples. It is a fact that compilation error messages have often been considered to be wholly inadequate, and yet tolerated. This is pointless; although the software engineer may appreciate the difficulty of producing meaningful error messages from the complex task of analysing the source text, it behoves him/her to complain loudly if the results do not facilitate the task for which the tool is intended.

On some computer systems the successful completion of the compilation process will automatically execute the produced object code by default; on others, the execution of the produced code requires a separate command. A separate command will invariably be provided on all systems, however, since it allows previously compiled code to be executed without going through the compilation process each time.

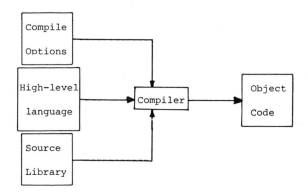

Fig 8.1 The process of compilation

Figure 8.1 illustrates a simple compilation process. The source library is a collection of routines written and stored in the high-level language in use, and their incorporation in the final code will be achieved by means of a simple statement in the main program specifying which routines are to be used.

Compile options can be supplied either embedded within the source program (program options), to apply locally to a section of program, or as part of the operating system command which calls the compiler into action, in which case they have a global affect on the whole of the compilation. Examples of program options would be list/nolist commands which result in certain sections of the program not being listed, or an index_check/ no_index_check pair which will cause or inhibit code being produced to carry out checks on array bounds being exceeded. A compile option might specify the type of error listing to be produced (e.g. full, error lines only) or that all run-time checks (array indexes, subranges) be turned on/off.

8.3.2.2 Independent Compilation

The 'object code' could be in executable form as we have seen, but a much more flexible translation system is provided if this is not the case. The generation of pure machine code is possible only if the whole source program is supplied to the compiler. But, as we have seen throughout the book, software engineering principles will see a complex program broken down into small modules each of which will be validated separately before being combined with other modules. The capability for independent compilation at the module level gives the flexibility that is needed.

Object code with such a system, therefore, will be in some intermediate form - a halfway stage, if you like, between the high-level language and the final machine-code equivalent. One possibility for a intermediate form is a recognisable assembly language. This has a couple of advantages. For one thing, it means that the compiler output can be modified by hand at a later stage - if key areas needed increased efficiency for performance reasons (see chapter 7). The other benefit is that such a system would facilitate the inclusion of assembly language sections in the high-level program. Figure 8.2 illustrates the process.

Given the software engineering difficulties associated with assembly language programming, this is not necessarily an approach that will commend itself in all cases; for an application which unavoidably requires a small amount of low-level work, however, this may be the best solution.

Whatever the form of the object code, independent compilation will produce a collection cf routines in this intermediate form. This collection has to be integrated at some stage so as to form a complete program. This task of 'program building' is discussed in section 8.4.

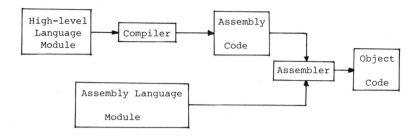

Fig 8.2 Compilation via assembly language

8.3.3 COMPILER STANDARDS AND VALIDATION

A high-level language, apart from providing the programmer with a convenient and powerful notation, has the immense advantage that it is machine
independent. Unlike assembly language, which is necessarily based upon the
architecture of a particular brand of computer, a high-level language has
no such constraint. Pascal is Pascal is Pascal. A Pascal program written
and developed using a compiler on one machine, should successfully compile
under a Pascal compiler on another machine. The portability of high-level
language programs from one machine to another is thus assured, with much
saving in time and effort.

Mostly theory, unfortunately. Compilers produced by computer manufacturers
can be quite different, even though they are based on the same high-level
language. The upshot of this situation is that a Pascal program, say, for
machine X has to be modified - possibly extensively - before it will work
on machine Y with its compiler for a different dialect of Pascal. Nobody
benefits from this stupidity except the computer/compiler manufacturers,
with users being tied to their particular products because of the volume
of rework needed to move elsewhere.

Enter the Standard. From chapter 7 it will be remembered that programming
languages have always been associated with definitions of what constituted
a legal program in that language - the ALGOL definition, for instance. But
this definition has too often been seen as the starting point, with either
additions or deletions to this definition being made by individual imple-
mentors of compilers for that language: hence the anarchic situation described above. A standard goes that bit further. It is an acceptance, by a
recognised standards authority, that such-and-such a definition of a high-
level language is to be regarded as the standard for compilers for that
language. The American National Standards Institute (ANSI) is such an organisation, and ANSI standards now exist for the major languages. Stndards
do not solve the problem, however, but they do force compiler writers to
at least define the ways in which their implementations diverge from the
accepted standard.

Taken one step further, Compiler Validation, is the result of the worm at
least starting to turn. A user will specify, as one of the non-functional

requirements for software to be produced on his behalf, that software be written in a language for which the compiler has been validated: that is, confirmed by some independent organisation to conform to the standard for that language. In this way the customer can be sure that compatibility is assured at least between different software products produced on their behalf, even though compatibilty with other users could not be guaranteed unless they, too, had been as forward-thinking.

Paradoxically, the proliferation of small software houses is starting to help in this direction. By ensuring that their products are validated such houses are starting to pick up business from those larger organisations who attempt to remain outside the validation requirement.

Typically a compiler validation will result in a report which sets out the observed results from a series of tests designed to demonstrate that compiler's adherence, or lack of it, to the language standard. For instance, the National Computing Centre validation for COBOL compilers involves 300 programs, each of which comprise several individual tests. Successfully validated products will be certificated and added to a list of compilers which have current validation certificates; a sensible customer will ask for software to be compiled using one of the entries on such a list.

8.4 Program Building

8.4.1 THE REQUIREMENT

We have seen that it is desirable to be able to write a program in modules and to compile those modules independently in order to iron out any syntax errors; that, in working in this way, it is easy for a change in any small part of the whole program to be effected quickly by simply editing and re-compiling the faulty module rather than the whole, probably substantial, program.

In addition, independent compilation allows the construction of libraries of pre-compiled modules which can be incorporated into a program. Routines which are of use to a large number of programs are written and fully tested. They are then compiled, the object modules being stored in what is termed an object library file on disc; from here they can be added to a program without having to be compiled again.

This approach is regularly employed with the 'run-time library' for a language system. With Pascal, for instance, the actual implementation of input/output commands like READ, READLN, WRITE, WRITELN etc. will be machine dependent, unavoidably. By holding the object code for these functions in a separate library file, they can aid the portability of the program by having the correct routines for the hardware configuration in use added in a way that does not require changes to the source program.

Similarly, some compiler run-time options (the Pascal Profiler in chapter 9, for instance) will be implemented by means of augmenting the compiled source program object modules with additional compiled code to carry out the particular run-time function.

Although not widely used, mixed-language programming - that is, writing parts of a program in one high-level language and parts in another, the idea being that the most suitable language can be chosen for implementing individual modules - depends on the different language compilers producing compatible object modules which are then combined to form the complete program.

Finally, as an alternative to that seen in 8.3.2.2 above, a convenient way of adding assembly language routines to a program is to write them as independent routines, assemble them into compatible object code to that being produced by the high-level language compiler, and then join them together.

'Joining them together', combining a number of object modules so as to form a complete program, is therefore a major requirement for the software engineer. The tool employed for this task is the Link Editor.

8.4.2 LINK EDITOR

Figure 8.3 illustrates the basic process of link editing. A collection of object modules, either user-generated as the product of compilation or held within the system object libary, are passed by means of an operating system command to the Link Editor. The editor (sometimes known as a link loader) combines these routines to form a single file of machine-code for subsequent execution. Various options can usually be specified as part of the link editor invocation, such as whether or not listings are required, the form they should take etc.

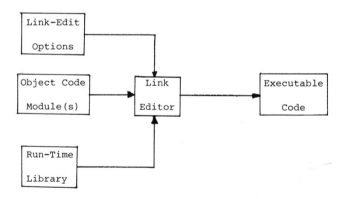

Fig. 8.3 Program building

The two major functions of the link editor are:

Collection: resolving cross-references between the routines;

Mapping: the assignment of actual memory addresses to the executable code.

These are best illustrated by means of a simple example.

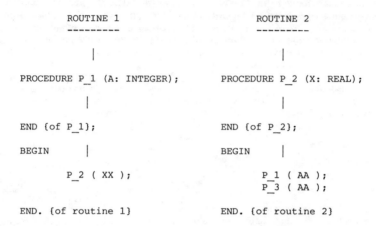

```
        ROUTINE 1                      ROUTINE 2
        ---------                      ---------

            |                              |

PROCEDURE P_1 (A: INTEGER);    PROCEDURE P_2 (X: REAL);

            |                              |

END {of P_1};                  END {of P_2};

BEGIN       |                  BEGIN       |

      P_2 ( XX );                    P_1 ( AA );
                                     P_3 ( AA );

      END. {of routine 1}       END. {of routine 2}
```

These two routines are to be combined by the link editor. They have been independently compiled, so the object code for routine 1 will have within it a reference to procedure P_2 which is 'unsatisfied' - that is, the compiler was unable to locate the procedure in order to convert the call of P_2 into its machine-code equivalent. The same thing applies to the call of P_1 in routine 2.

These are examples of cross references between the two routines which the link editor has to sort out. It does this by reading - collecting - the routines one by one into memory, noting the appearance of routines that have been referred to earlier and backtracking to complete the machine-code translation which could only be partially carried out by the compiler.

At the end of this process, any unsatisfied references which still remain must be reported as errors. The call in routine 2 of the non-existent P_3 procedure is an example of the error that is detected by the link editor. Correcting such errors requires a change to the source program, of course, and that means re-compilation.

Address mapping is also a function of the link editor. Compilation of an individual routine can do no more than translate variables into memory addresses on the basis of the routine being located at, normally, address zero onwards. When two or more such routines are combined, the addresses in the object code of all but the first routine have to be changed to reflect their actual positions relative to the start of the whole program. By tracking and converting the address parts of instructions as each of the routines is collected, this function is also carried out by a link editor. (Note that this is not the end of the address saga; a further relocation of addresses may well have to take place when the whole program is finally located in the computer memory at run-time).

When calling the link editor into action, then, the order in which the routines are named may well be important, since it determines the order in which the routines will be physically located in memory. Typically there will be a 'store map' listing generated which gives the names of each of the routines that have been linked together and their relative positions. Cross-references will also be detailed together with the positions at which they appear. This information is crucial (see 6.2.3) since it gives evidence of the latest build state for the whole software package.

8.5   Summary

* Like any other engineer, the software engineer needs tool to do the job in hand; editors, translators and program builder⌐ comprise the basic tool-kit for a software engineer.

* Editors come in two flavours: line editors and screen editors. There is no comparison between the two, with a screen editor being vastly superior.

* Translation of a source program can be achieved by an interpreter or compiler. An interpreter, apart from the benefits of immediacy, has few advantages. Compilers provide considerably more flexibility as regards structured programming techniques.

* The validation of a compiler - that it meets a defined standard for a language implementation - should be the norm, and sought by software engineers as a matter of course.

* Program building enables the integration of a number of independently compiled modules to form a complete program. This is an essential tool for modular program development.

8.6   Things to Think About

* What would be a minimal function set for a line editor? How would this set differ from that required with a screen editor? What is the cost in system terms for the additional capability of the latter?

* Could an interpreter be written for a language such as Pascal? If so, what would be its main limitations?

* Why should such things as compile options exist? Why not incorporate every diagnostic feature automatically?

* Evaluate the benefits of having a validation process for English as taught in our schools!

* Is program building necessary for a self-contained program? Why not incorporate run-time routines at compile time?

CHAPTER NINE

Testing and Debugging: Techniques and Tools

"Detection is, or ought to be, an exact science, and
should be treated in the same cold and unemotional
manner. You have attempted to tinge it with romanticism, which produces much the same effect as if you
worked a love-story or an elopement into the fifth
proposition of Euclid."

Sir Arthur Conan Doyle,
The Sign of Four (A Sherlock Holmes story)

9.1 Introduction

Sherlock Holmes didn't always get it right. In this chapter, as we look at
the various approaches to testing and debugging programs, we will discover
that the occasional touch of Watsonian romanticism is not a bad thing to
have around.

Our faithful old Telephone Directory System (TDS) will once again be used
as the basis for discussion. Figure 9.1 gives a slightly more detailed
design for a this system, with the MODIFY part of the program having been
expanded.

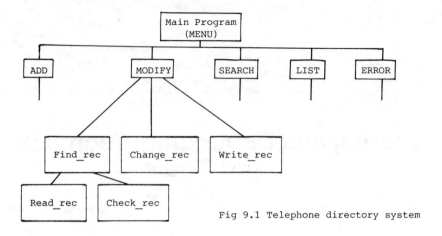

Fig 9.1 Telephone directory system

The lower level routines carry out the following operations:

Find_rec: find the nominated record in the database
Change_rec: change this record as required
Write_rec: write the new record back to the database

Read_rec: read a record from disc
Check_rec: check this record to see if it's the one wanted

9.2   Principles of Testing

9.2.1 TOP-DOWN AND BOTTOM-UP TESTING

The application of a sound design methodology will result in a software design which comprises a hierarchy of modules, sub-modules and units. The techniques of top-down and bottom-up testing both reflect such a hierarchy in their use.

Bottom-up testing (sometimes referred to in a faintly derogatory manner as the 'classical approach' to testing) involves the testing of individual elements first, followed by the integration testing of combined elements. In this way testing proceeds from the bottom of the design upwards. Thus for TDS, testing in a bottom-up fashion would mean that Check_rec and Read_rec were tested individually, then combined with Find_rec and that little conglomerate tested. Change_rec and Write_rec would be dealt with in the same way before being combined with MODIFY.

Testing a unit will require the additional development of a test harness, or driver, program. The driver effectively acts as part of the calling routine, exercising interfaces and sending and/or receiving test data and results.

The main disadvantages of bottom-up testing are as follows:

* Because testing of the complete system is, by definition, only carried out in the final stages, major design flaws do not show up until late in the day; inevitably the resolution of such errors will require some reworking (and thus retesting) of lower level routines.

* There is no visible, working system until the later stages of testing; pressures may build up which lead to testing being skimped in order to have something to 'show' the customer/management.

Top-down testing (a 'modern' technique) does not just work in the opposite direction; it necessarily dictates that testing and programming are dealt with side-by-side, modules being tested immediately after they are written and before the programming of their subordinate modules. The maxim "build a little, test a little" applies. Developing TDS in top-down fashion would mean that MENU was written and tested before MODIFY and the other routines at the same level had started to come along; Find_rec, Change_rec and Write_rec would be developed only when MODIFY had been satisfactorily dealt with, and so on.

A snapshot of top-down development for TDS during the testing of find_rec, therefore, might look that of figure 9.2:

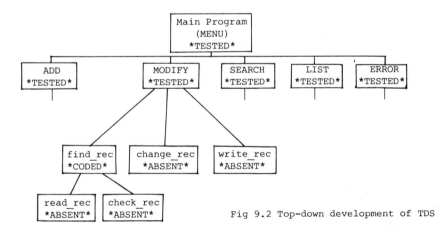

Fig 9.2 Top-down development of TDS

Now on the face of it there appears to be a problem. How is it possible to test Find_rec without having the routines, Read_rec and Check_rec, that it calls? Similarly, how can we claim that MODIFY has been tested? The answer is that those items in figure 9.2 indicated as *ABSENT* are actually present in the form of 'stubs': surrogate pieces of code which are replaced as and when the real thing is developed.

Stubs have to be written of course, with their action ranging from that of a more-or-less simple simulation of the routine they represent down to the generation of nothing more than a 'Kilroy was here'-like message.

The major advantages of top-down testing overcome the disadvantages of bottom-up testing:

* Top-level design flaws are revealed quickly since the higher levels of the hierarchy are tested first; for the most part, errors detected do not require other routines to be recoded. After any correction is made re-testing of all existing elements is carried out automatically.

* A working version is produced very quickly. Aside from the benefits of being able to prove to management that something is actually happening these top-level implementations can demonstrate flaws in the require- ments specification when the customer realises that his wishes have been wrongly interpreted.

Top-down testing does have its disadvantages, however, and these - you've guessed it - are the advantages of the bottom-up approach.

* A software implementation will often have a few modules at a low level in its design hierarchy which are 'critical' for some reason - because they relate to performance or a key algorithm, for instance. Read_rec might be such a module in TDS if the structure of the directory file on disc was particularly complicated. Using a strict top-down approach difficulties with critical modules would only be discovered towards the end of testing; this would obviously not be so with the bottom-up approach.

* Low-level modules are also quite often concerned with input/output. In bottom-up development and testing these modules will quickly be avail- able; top-down testing might well require widespread use of specially planted instructions at intermediate levels in order to generate test results.

In practice then, a good old British compromise can often be an effective way forward. Top-down testing using stubs will be the predominant method employed, but with critical routines being written and tested in parallel through the use of test drivers. Naturally this mixed approach should not just happen; the existence of special cases should have been identified at detailed design, and the strategy for their testing outlined in the Test Plan.

9.2.2 RATIONALE

9.2.2.1 Black-box and White-box Testing

In simple terms, a test is conducted on a section of code. That section

162

may be a single, lowly item in the software hierarchy (e.g. Read_rec in
TDS) or a group of code modules being tested en masse (e.g. MODIFY and all
its subordinate routines) but ultimately the test should be concerned with
either what that section does, or how it does it.

'What' testing is known as black-box testing. The section under test will
be known to perform certain functions in response to certain inputs. It
will also be known to produce certain outputs, and to affect known global
data items. A black-box test, therefore, will concentrate on the interface
between the code section and its surroundings.

'How' testing is known as white-box testing. Details of internal workings
of the code section - data structures used, code paths and loops employed
so as to achieve the functional performance - are known; a white box test
uses this knowledge to exercise code specifics in an attempt to uncover
flaws in the program logic.

As the methods are complementary, a code section should be tested through
both black- and white-box techniques.

9.2.2.2 Design of Test Cases

A test case is a design for a particular test. It will stipulate criteria
for the generation of test data, the criteria being tailored according to
whether a black- or white-box test is being conducted.

The following are the most common approaches to test case design:

Path (or Logic) Testing

A white-box technique, its objective is to cause the traversal of a
number of different paths through the code under test. Naturally the
degree to which this is possible will depend on the complexity of the
coding, but general objectives might be:

* execution of every statement at least once;
* every decision path taken for true and false conditions;

The difficulty of path testing is obviously exacerbated the more
complex the code under test. It may be necessary in practice for the
strategy to identify a representative sample of paths if the number of
possible combinations is unrealistically high.

Path testing is equally applicable to module and integration tests, in
the latter case the paths being the links between modules.

Note that, of itself, path testing does not prove that a program will
produce the right results. If a path is missing it cannot be traversed
by the test although its absence will cause incorrect results at some
time. Path testing should be combined with meaningful data wherever it
is possible.

Boundary and Stress Testing

This technique tests software at its operational extremes. It is based
on the principle that many errors occur at the upper and lower points
of a range, and thus aims to test data structures, control flows, and
data values just below, at, and just above their supposed maxima and
minima. Boundary testing can be used in a variety of situations, both
in black-box and white-box testing. For example:

Black-box: creating empty and full file structures;
                  input of out-of-range data values, including null input;
                  attempting invalid operations e.g. edit non-existent file.

White box: array handling with subscripts outside declared range;
                 loops which are executed zero, maximum times;
                 values for variables with defined limits.

In a similar fashion, boundary testing can be used to obtain a measure
of performance capability. The multi-user TDS, for instance, would be
tested with the loading of terminal users and data rates stated in the
requirements specification and the system performance measured.

Stress testing, as its name suggests, is performance boundary testing
carried to the point at which the software 'gives way'. If the number
of on-line TDS terminals was continually increased the system response
time would gradually, then rapidly, degrade. Stress testing would aim
to discover the values associated with this degredation.

Equivalence (Input Data) Partitioning

A black-box technique, its objective is to kill a number of birds with
one stone by defining test cases which uncover classes, as opposed to
individual, errors.

A primary target for this sort of test is the data structure and the
coding which manipulates it. By selection of a combination of invalid
and valid data sets for input to the routine under test it is argued
that a good chance exists for a small group of tests, applied repeatedly to uncover a number of errors.

9.2.2.3 Regression Testing

Although not strictly a technique in itself, regression tests do exercise
the mind during the testing phases of the software life-cycle. As we have
said repeatedly, a successful test will uncover errors. These errors are
then corrected, and regression - 'going back' - tests are then carried out
on the modified software.

The question to be answered is: how far back do the tests have to go? At
the extreme, every test ever conducted on the item of software in
question would be repeated; in practice it is usually possible to justify

with some confidence a regression test which is a subset of those carried out before. Given that the software is well structured it should really only be necessary to retest the amended module and its interfaces anyway.

Once again, the Test Plan should provide guidelines for regression testing related to the software design.

9.3 Testing Techniques

9.3.1 STRUCTURED WALKTHROUGHS

If you're looking for the bit on how to write test programs you'll have to wait for a while. Whilst test software will inevitably be needed in some capacity, the test theories outlined above need not be solely implemented by generating more programs (which have to be tested, by the way). A very successful method of finding errors doesn't involve getting anywhere near a computer at all.

A structured walkthrough (or code inspection) is a review meeting (see chapter 6) with differences. The 'structured' bit isn't one of them; the term is merely an indication that, like a review meeting, the session shouldbe well organised with a chairman, a secretary and a clearly defined agenda. The principle differences are:

* the object to be 'walked-through', under review if you prefer, is an item of some detail - an aspect of detailed design or, more usually, a piece of program coding.

* the group will comprise peer group staff for the person whose work is being scrutinised: at this level, programmers and analysts. Since the objective of the walkthrough is to be the discovery of errors it is seen to be psychologically important that these people are non-threatening, i.e. non-management!

* In this respect the members of the group will be expected to take on different roles (such as user, program maintainer, quality assurance representative) for the purposes of the meeting.

As with a design review, a structured walkthrough will begin with a presentation of the work by the programmer author. During this explanation the other members of the group will intervene as necessary to ask for further clarification, or to make constructive criticisms. The walkthrough seeks to identify errors, but not to correct them: that is the programmer's job. It also looks at areas which, although not erroneous in themselves, either contravene sound programming practices or presage future trouble.

The following is a typical checklist of points to be considered during a structured walkthrough:

* Does the coded unit implement all the functions of the detailed design specification?
  [this particular exercise, apart from serving the obvious purpose, can also highlight deficiencies in the structuring of the program if it is found that individual functions cannot be clearly traced]

* Is it easy to cross-refer to the detailed design specification?
  [somebody else may have to do this one day; examination helps to ease the problems of future maintenance]

* Are there any logical coding errors?
  [these will often be discovered by the programmer, simply through the process of explaining how the program works. In this respect a major benefit of the walkthrough is that many errors may be uncovered in a single session, rather than through test runs taking place over a relatively long period of time]

* Is the programming 'defensive' and has this been tested for?
  [has the programmer included checks for errors which may occur during the execution of the program? These include error conditions specified in the requirements, together with 'internal' checks for particular occurrences, e.g. division by zero. It is human - well, programmer - nature to leave these checks until later .. much later]

* Is the program commented adequately?
  [which can extend to a walkthrough of any associated documentation if this is appropriate]

* Have any obscure methods or code been used?
  ['trick', or unnecessarily complex, programming is to be deplored: a development programmer's high will almost certainly be a maintenance programmer's low at some future - inconvenient - time]

* Has the programmer justified the use of any low-level code inserts?
  [as we have seen in Chapter 7, machine- or assembly-language coding is a form of obscure programming that will sometimes have to be employed - but only for good reason]

9.3.2 WRITING TEST DRIVERS AND STUBS

The use of test drivers and stubs in top-down and bottom-up testing was introduced in 9.2.1 above. Although their mode of application differs, it is important to recognise that both drivers and stubs are serving a common cause, namely the implementation of a test case.

A test driver invokes the piece of code to be tested. Before doing so it must initialise any data values that that code uses, either by statements within the driver, or by reading the data from some external source. When the code under test has been obeyed, return is made to the driver which has to verify - usually by printing/displaying data items - that functions have been carried out correctly.

166

As a simple illustration, the following code is an outline black-box test driver for the Find_rec component of TDS (written in pseudo-BBC BASIC):

```
10      NAM$="TESTNAME": TEL$="TESTTELNO"
20        REM *Initialise global variables to dummy values*
30      Name$="FRED"
40        REM *Initialise input parameter*
50      PROCFind_rec(Name$):
60        REM *Call the code to be tested*
70      IF Result=TRUE PRINT Name$,NAM$,TEL$ ELSE PRINT "No Match"
80        REM *Display results on return from code*
90      END

1000      DEFPROCFind_rec(N$)
1010      REPEAT
1020        PROCRead_rec
1030          REM *gets next NAM$,TEL$ from serial file*
1040          REM *sets end_of_file=TRUE if at end of file*
1050        PROCCheck_rec(N$,NAM$)
1060          REM *sets result on comparison of N$,NAM$*
1070      UNTIL Result=TRUE OR end-of-file
```

A test stub takes the place of an as yet uncoded routine in the software hierarchy. On a variety of occasions, therefore, the stub will be called into action by a routine which is being tested. Minimally, the stub must appear externally identical to the routine that will eventually replace it - parametric information must be received and transmitted, if only in the form of dummy values. At the other extreme, a stub could take the form of a complex simulation of the routine it is representing, e.g. by producing database information instead of reading it from disc.

The stub, when called into action, must accept any data passed to it and pass back any data expected from it. Some indication will normally occur to indicate that the stub has been entered: a data transformation will take place and/or some output message generated.

The following shows simple Read_rec and Check_rec stubs for use in the testing of Find_rec:

```
10      DEFPROCFind_rec(N$): REM N$ produced by MODIFY
20      REPEAT
30        PROCRead_rec
40          REM *gets next NAM$,TEL$ from serial file*
50          REM *sets end_of_file=TRUE if at end of file*
60        PROCCheck_rec(N$,NAM$)
70          REM *sets result on comparison of N$,NAM$*
80      UNTIL Result=TRUE OR end-of-file

1000      DEFPROCRead_rec
1010      PRINT"READ_REC ENTERED"
```

```
1020      REM *'Here I am' message*
1030    NAM$="FRED"
1040    TEL$="01-424-9999"
1050    end-of-file=FALSE
1060      REM *Global variables set to something*
1070    PRINT"EXIT FROM READ_REC"
1080      REM *'There I was' message*
1090    ENDPROC


2000    DEFPROCCheck_rec(N$,NAM$): LOCAL R%
2010    PRINT"CHECK_REC ENTERED"
2020    PRINT"DATA: ";N$,NAM$
2030      REM *Entry message + output of parameters*
2040    R%=RND(10): Result=R%<5:
2050      REM *Set result TRUE/FALSE at random*
2060    PRINT"result= ";Result
2070    PRINT"EXIT FROM CHECK_REC"
2080      REM *print result and exit message*
2090    ENDPROC
```

9.4   Tools for Testing

Testing requires a lot of effort; computers are supposed to save effort. It therefore makes a lot of sense to look at ways in which computer-based aids - tools - can be employed with the testing of software.

There is another reason: that good testing tools should help the tester to do a better job. Tightening wheel-nuts by hand will produce a far bumpier ride than doing the same task with the aid of a good socket set: the same principle applies to the use software tools.

We will consider just a few examples of the wide (and growing much wider, as Chapter 10 indicates) range of tools available, concentrating on the two broad categories known as Static and Dynamic Analysers.

9.4.1 STATIC ANALYSERS

Static analysis involves the examination of programs without their being executed. Thus a structured walkthrough could be classified as a static analysis technique. A static analysis tool will operate primarily by means of inspecting program source code structure and syntax so as to highlight errors and produce statistical information for the programmer to use.

The compiler is the most common form of static analyser, albeit with the analyis part carried out as a by-product from the main task of translation from high-level language to object code. If the compiler extends its range to include some inspection of the source code, errors other than those purely to do with incorrect syntax can be detected. The following shows a compiler listing for a do-nothing Pascal program:

```
Pascal-2 RSX V2.1A   23-JUL-86   10:03 AM

    1   PROGRAM TEST(INPUT, OUTPUT);
    2     VAR
    3        A, B, C, D: INTEGER;
    4        TF: BOOLEAN;
    5     PROCEDURE ONE(ALPHA, BETA: INTEGER;
    6              VAR GAMMA: REAL);              {Change to  .. : INTEGER);}
    7     BEGIN
    8        WRITELN('ONE ENTERED');
    9        GAMMA = ALPHA + BETA;               {Change to  GAMMA := ..}
                   ^33
*** 33: ':=' EXPECTED

   10        WRITELN('EXIT FROM ONE')
   11        END {ONE};
   12     PROCEDURE TWO(ALPHA, BETA: INTEGER;
   13           VAR LOGICAL: BOOLEAN);
   14     BEGIN
   15        WRITELN('TWO ENTERED');
   16        IF ALPHA > BETA THEN
   17          LOGICAL := TRUE
   18        ELSE
   19          LOGICAL := FALSE;
   20        WRITELN('EXIT FROM TWO')
   21        END {TWO};
   22     BEGIN
   23                                  {Insert  A := 10;}
   24        B := 20;
   25        ONE(A, B, C);
              ^137  ^92
*** 137: MUST ASSIGN VALUE BEFORE USING VARIABLE
***  92: ACTUAL PARAMETER TYPE DOESN'T MATCH FORMAL PARAMETER TYPE

   33        TWO(20, B, TF);
   34        TWO(15, B, TF);
   35        TWO(10, B, TF);
   36     END.
```

The error in line 9 is obviously syntactical. Those detected in line 25, however, are the result of static analysis. Although not syntactically wrong in itself, line 25 has been flagged as being an 'error line'. This can be misleading since, in this case, the source of both errors happens to be elsewhere: the statement to initialise variable A is missing (line 23), and variable GAMMA in procedure ONE has been declared as INTEGER when it should have been REAL.

A good compiler, or separate static analysis package, could pick up other error (or potential error) conditions such as infinite loops, unreachable statements, improperly nested loops and unused variables.

Another static analysis tool is the Cross-Referencer. This produces for a given program a summary of variables   declared, and the locations in the program at which they are initialised and used.   By using such a table of cross-references in conjunction with the program listing errors which have escaped detection by the compiler can be picked up. A cross-reference listing for the 'corrected' form of the previous Pascal program is given below:

```
CROSS REFERENCE:  * INDICATES DEFINITION, = INDICATES ASSIGNMENT

-A-
A           3*    23=    25
ALPHA       5*    9      12*    16

-B-
B           3*    24=    25     26    27    28
BETA        5*    9      12*    16
BOOLEAN     4     13

-C-
C           3*    25

-D-
D           3*

-F-
FALSE       19

-G-
GAMMA       6*    9=

-I-
INPUT       1*
INTEGER     3     5      6      12

-L-
LOGICAL     13*   17=    19=

-O-
ONE         5*    25
OUTPUT      1*

-T-
TEST        1*
TF          4*    26     27     28
TRUE        17
TWO         12*   26     27     28

-W-
WRITELN     8     10     15     20
```

As a simple example of the sort of potential error that can be picked up, note that the entry for variable D shows that it is declared in line 3 but never initialised. If variable D just happens not to be used then nothing, other than wasted storage space, is lost; if D should have been used else-where, but hasn't for some reason - perhaps a typing mistake - then the static analysis has unearthed an error.

9.4.2 DYNAMIC ANALYSIS

Dynamic analysis involves the production of information during, or after, the execution of the program being tested. Obviously the programmer can build a certain amount of dynamic self-analysis into a program by means of a liberal scattering of output statements into key areas. A compilation system which allows some statements to be included conditionally is very useful in this respect.

As regards externally conducted dynamic analysis, the tools most commonly employed are those involved with execution flow. We look at two examples - tracing and profiling.

9.4.2.1 Program Tracing

A trace facility will provide information about the sequence in which a program's statements were obeyed. This enables the programmer to evaluate the effectiveness of the test cases being used - for instance, to ensure that particular sets of test data cause the expected program paths to be taken.

The example below shows the output produced using the TRACE facility prov-ided through the BBC BASIC system: a summary of line numbers visited. The only option available is shown in the second run of the program. By using a line number with the TRACE ON call, the tracing can be limited to the main program - i.e. the procedure calls in a well-structured program.

```
10PROC_ROOT(1,2,1)
20PROC_ROOT(20,30,5)
30END

100DEFPROC_ROOT(B,E,I)
110LOCAL I%
120FOR I%=B TO E STEP I
130PRINT"SQROOT OF ";I%;" = ";SQR(I%)
140NEXT I%
150ENDPROC

>TRACE ON

>RUN
[10] [110] [120] [130] SQROOT OF 1 = 1
```

171

```
[140] SQROOT OF 2 = 1.41421356
[140] [150] [20] [110] [120] [130] SQROOT OF 20 = 4.47213596
[140] SQROOT OF 25 = 5
[140] SQROOT OF 30 = 5.47722557
[140] [150] [30]

>TRACE 100

>RUN

[10] SQROOT OF 1 = 1
SQROOT OF 2 = 1.41421356
[20] SQROOT OF 20 = 4.47213596
SQROOT OF 25 = 5
SQROOT OF 30 = 5.47722557
[30]
```

9.4.2.2 Program Execution Profile

An Execution Profiler is a tool which summarises the frequencies of execution of individual program statements during a program run. An example of
the output from this sort of package is given in below. The figures in the
left-hand column give the number of times that the statement on that line
was executed.

```
            Pascal-2 RSX V2.1A 23-JUL-86 10:21 AM

        COUNT  LINE STMT

                 1          PROGRAM TRIVIA(INPUT, OUTPUT);
                 2
                 3          VAR
                 4              C2, C3, C5: INTEGER;
                 5              I: INTEGER;
                 6
            1    7     1     BEGIN
            1    8     2         C2 := 0;
            1    9     3         C3 := 0;
            1   10     4         C5 := 0;
            1   11     5         FOR I := 1 TO 1000 DO
                12                 BEGIN
         1000   13     6         IF I MOD 2 = 0 THEN
          500   14     7             C2 := C2 + 1;
         1000   15     8         IF I MOD 3 = 0 THEN
          333   16     9             C3 := C3 ; 1;
         1000   17    10         IF I MOD 5 = 0 THEN
          200   18    11             C5 := C5 + 1
                19                 END;
            1   20    12         WRITELN(C2);
            1   21    13         WRITELN(C3);
            1   22    14         WRITELN(C5);
                23          END.
```

By reference to an execution profile it is possible to see immediately if
some statements are not being executed at all - indicating either a poor
test case, or parhaps a logical error which is preventing such statements
being executed.

Another use of a profile is in boundary testing for performance. If the
program needs to be speeded up, a knowledge of which statement groups are
called most frequently enables re-coding for maximising efficiency to be
accurately focussed.

9.5   Debugging

"How often have I said to you that when you have
eliminated the impossible, whatever remains,
however improbable, must be the truth?"

Sir Arthur Conan Doyle,
The Sign of Four (A Sherlock Holmes story)

Let's get the terminology clear to begin with: testing is about revealing
the presence of an error; debugging is about discovering the source of the
error, in order that it can be removed. Holmes' philosophy of debugging
illustrates the essential difficulty with the whole business - that finding out what is causing an error is something of an art: a mixture of
experience, knowledge, technique and, to be honest, the odd bit of luck.

Debugging tools can help in two ways: they can either provide information,
or else the wherewithal by which information can be gained. They cannot
debug, however, any more than a dictionary can solve a crossword puzzle;
that is down to the programmer's effective use of the tools.

The static and dynamic analysis tools mentioned before can obviously help
with debugging. Good compilation and run-time error messages are worth
their weight in line-printer paper. The compiler message for line 9 of
the example in 9.4.1 above is a simple instance of how the source of an
error can be clearly identified; those messages on line 25, however, only
indicate a symptom - the cure for which is found elsewhere.

Run-time error messages, coupled with a trace facility, can indicate the
nature of an error, the location at which it was detected, and provide an
audit trail of procedure calls if the error has occurred at a point some
way down in the hierarchical structure of the program. Again, however, the
actual source of the problem may be somewhere completely different.

Associated with traces might be some sort of dump facility. In its crudest
form, the dump would give the contents of individual registers and memory
addresses (a mandatory requirement of any TV high-tech drama is that Our

Hero should 'crack' such a dump). More usefully, a symbolic dump produces source-program related output by listing the final values of the program variables at the moment when the program stopped.

Used by experienced programmers the information from debugging tools such as these can provide the clues necessary to track down the source of the error. Their limitations should be fairly obvious, however. Using a memory dump to find out why a program came to a premature end is equivalent to examining a corpse to discover the cause of death: detection is possible, but it would be so much quicker to have seen it happen. Action-replay, in other words, is preferable to autopsy.

A dynamic debugger is a collection of routines which are appended to the program under test as part of the compile-and-link process. When the program is run, the debugger code is entered and controls the execution of the program by responding to commands input by the tester. In this situation, with diagnostic and trace information being generated when required, a skilled tester will be able to 'see' the events which lead to the untimely end of his beloved program.

The features of a typical debugger program would include the following:

Breakpoints

A breakpoint is a position, established within the program under test, at which, when reached, execution will be interrupted and control returned to the debugger. Thus the tester, by inserting breakpoints into strategic places, can force the program to pause whilst variable contents are examined. A range of commands will relate to the use of breakpoints:

* set/remove a breakpoint on an instruction
* set/remove a breakpoint on the use of a data item;
* continue execution after stopping at a breakpoint;
* display current breakpoint settings.

List

To control the output of debugging information, usually when stopped at a breakpoint:

* display procedure trace;
* display last N statements obeyed;
* list section of source code;
* list contents of named variables;

Controlled execution

To examine any intra-breakpoint part of the program in detail:

* single-step 1 statement;
* single-step N statements;

* proceed to the next breakpoint.

Used to full effect, these commands should enable the person carrying out
a program post-mortem to see when and where the poison is administered!

9.6   Summary

* A software hierarchy will be tested in either bottom-up or top-down
  fashion. Bottom-up testing is best employed for key routines, whilst
  top-down testing is used for testing the majority of the structure.

* Test cases should have either a white- or black-box rationale; path,
  boundary/stress and equivalence partitioning form a complementary set
  of test cases.

* A structured walkthrough enables code to be tested by scrutiny, and
  can lead to a number of errors being uncovered in a single session.

* A programmed implementation of a test case will require either test
  drivers (for bottom-up testing) or test stubs (top-down) to be coded.

* Tools for testing can assist with either static or dynamic analysis;
  static analysis provides information on a program before execution,
  dynamic analysis during execution.

* Debuggin involves find the source of an error and correcting it. A
  debugging tool can be particularly useful in this respect.

9.7   Things to Think About

* Consider the merits of the proposition that bottom-up testing should
  only be used in exceptional circumstances.

* Would a perfect series of black-box tests eliminate the need for any
  white-box testing? How about vice-versa?

* Frankenstein believes that his monster is now working perfectly - in
  particular, that he can dig a grave to any nominated dimensions. Come
  up with a suitable test case (presumably black-box).

* Try a structured walkthrough on one of your programs with some student
  colleagues. How would the atmosphere have been different had one of
  your tutors been present?

* Examine the manufacturer's documentation for any programming language
  that you use, and discover the full range of tools for static and/or
  dynamic analysis that are available. Go on then, try them out!

CHAPTER TEN

Future Developments in Software Engineering

"The future is not what it was"

Attr. by Bernard Levin to anonymous
professor of economics, Sunday Times, May 1977.

10.1   Formal Design Methods

The term 'formal' has been introduced into the software engineer's vocabulary to stress the importance of 'well formed' practices, as opposed to the apparently ad hoc approaches that have been adopted since the early days of software development. In this way it is intended to reflect the need for a method of software development which is underpinned by scientific and theoretic principles. Recent developments in 'formal methods', therefore, have been directed towards the possibility of treating the specification, design and implementation of software on a mathematical basis with formal analytical procedures.

Any formal method requires the existence of a mathematically-based model which represents both the individual objects and its operational behaviour for a given application. There also needs to be a calculus for the manipulation of the objects and their behaviour. In particular there needs to be a manipulation mechanism which supports the composition and decomposition of the objects thereby accommodating the refinement of the various levels of abstraction. In this way it is possible to provide a mechanism which supports the refinement process by assuring that correctness properties outlined in the specification are present in the design, and during each subsequent refinement step.

Formal methods play an important role throughout the development process. They can be used by designers to comparatively assess design alternatives; by software writers to precisely describe the system being built and to verify the software actually produced; by technical authors who have responsibility for the preparation of manuals; by test engineers in establishing suitable testing strategies for component testing and integration testing.

There are basically two categories of formal method: model-oriented and property-oriented. With model-oriented approaches, software specifications and designs are constructed directly using well-defined primitives. Examples of this approach include the Vienna Development Method and Z (Jackson(1985), Abrial(1982)). With a property-oriented approach, software specifications are formulated in terms of axioms which define the relationships of operations to each other. Interesting properties of the specifications can be deduced by logical manipulation of the axioms. The best-known approach is that involving algebraic specification of abstract data types (Goguen(1977)). This work is often presented in a very theoretical style although there are other axiomatic approaches which are presented in a rather more pragmatic way. Logic programming is such an approach, of which Prolog (Kowalski(1979)) is an example.

There are many arguments supporting the use of formal methods, not least of which is the increase in a project's manageability. Because inputs and outputs of each development stage are more clearly defined with a formal method, verification becomes less of an art and more of a science. It also provides a much sounder contractual basis for negotiations between customer and developer. Establishing a basis upon which precise definitions of software specification and design can be made is only half the battle, however. Unless this work is supported with the tools and development environments needed to assist in the complex areas of design and verification, little or no progress will be made in the practical, as opposed to theoretical, application of formal methods within industry.

10.2   Programming Languages for Software Engineering

Those responsible for the construction of large, complex software systems, such as real-time or embedded systems, frequently encounter problems which are not easily solved using existing development methods. These problems are partially attributable to:

* The size and complxity of the system being considered.

* The inability to monitor the real-time behaviour of a complex concurrent processing system.

* The lack of reliability associated with difficulties in producing an accurate specification of the requirements of the system, which results in implementation errors at a later date.

There is very little that can be done about the first of these, except to say that adequate managerial procedures should be introduced to reflect the inherent complexities. The second category of problem should be addressed by the support tools provided within the sophisticated programming support environments (see 10.3 below). The third is a prime target for solution through the use of formal specification languages.

A lack of reliability can be due to many things - ranging from programmer incompetence to the inadequate specification of the requirements. Too often the major cause is attributed to the latter. As highlighted in Chapter 3, the informal specification of requirements often results in a series of statements which is too vague to be used as a basis for the design, let alone as a contractual document.

A formal specification is essentially a model of the proposed system which attempts to reflect the system's behaviour as required by the user. Emphasis is given to 'what' it should do rather than 'how' it should do it. Its correctness is vital to the remaining development stages, for it is this that ensures that the behavioural properties are sound before proceeding to the next stage. Much of this work is still subject to considerable research at the time of writing. A brief description of a formal specification language, Z, is given for demonstrative purposes.

Z (Abrial(1982), Morgan(1984), Sorenson(1982)) is a specification language developed by the Programming Research Group at Oxford University. The basis of its notation is elementary set theory. The specification is written as a combination of formal Z and informal explanatory text written in English. In order to enhance the readability of the text the convention adopted is to surround the formal part in Z by boxes. The use of both formal and informal texts are intended to complement each other; the terseness of the formal part alone would dissuade users, and from bitter experience the informal part is far too vague to be used on its own. Great emphasis is placed upon the style and structure of the specification.

The objective with Z is to provide a means by which a system can be specified at a high level of abstraction, thereby avoiding implementation details. Decomposing the specification into a small number of modules enables the operation of the overall system to be visualised without resorting to the full-bodied monolithic description.

The vehicle used to organise and present the mathematical text of a Z specification is called a schema. Its general form is

```
┌─ Name ──────────────────────────────────
│
│   Variable declarations
│
│  ─────────────────────────────
│
│   Predicates
│
└──────────────────────────────────────────
```

The declarations are generally of the form

                identifier : type

the predicates giving the properties of the variables and the relat-

ionships between them. A schema may be used to describe either a state or
an operation. The state of the system is described using the declared
variables so as to form the components of the state, whilst the predicates
are used to derive the invariant properties of the state. To describe an
operation the variable declaration part is used to specify the initial and
final state components and the inputs and outputs; the predicate part
describes the relationship between them.

For further reading on the uses of Z see Hayes(1985).

10.3   Programming Support Environments

There are invariably two types of system in existence during the development of a software based project: a resident system, used on a frequent
basis for software development and training in the existing tools; and
the system which is being developed on behalf of the customer. These are
respectively known as the host and target machines. The inherent
incompatibilities between the high level of development tools that are
desirable on a host, and those that are expected to be provided on the
target, necessitate the provision of a host machine. Amongst the reasons
for supporting a host machine are the following:

* the target machine doesn't have sufficient hardware resources to support the necessary software development tools

* the target machine specification is such that it has insufficient processing power to support an operating system which will in turn provide the data handling capabilities that are necessary for the software
  development

* the target system operating system specification may not include the
  necessary facilities for such development requirements as process
  scheduling, efficient input/output primitives, or appropriate communication mechanisms

Additional facilities to those outlined in chapter 8 are going to be essential as the complexity of software increases. The areas of application
of these tools can also be extended to all aspects of the software
development process. For example, tools are required in the areas of software specification, verification and documentation. As a consequence of
the extension of its uses the phrase Programming Support Environment has
been coined to reflect the general capabilities of this host machine
software development work-horse.

A typical programming support environment would provide:

* Requirement specification and analysis facilities.

* Configuration management tools.

* General project planning facilities to assist in budgeting, critical
  path analysis, etc.

* Testing and fault diagnostic aids. Although these are akin to the tools mentioned in chapters 8 and 9, they are envisaged here as being far more sophisticated. This is particularly relevant when designing suitable test environments, where target machine simulators may have to be generated.

* Communication facilities to provide the basics necessary for both human and computer communication. This is particularly important for projects whose development is distributed over a wide geographical region. Electronic mail facilities which are having an impact on the day-to-day running of businesses, are a case in point. The likelihood is that their usage will increase as the resources become available.

  Host to target computer communication is equally vital in transferring the produced code prior to its execution, and monitoring its effect during run-time. General computer communication (or networking as it is sometimes called) is also important in that software and its supportive documents may be transferred between programming teams. All this significantly contributes towards the ease with which customer acceptance is achieved.

* Text processing facilities which include word processing and document maintenance capability. The latter is often overlooked, or dismissed as not being essential. This is unfortunate since documentation is one of the most important aspects of the software development process. It also happens to be quite an expensive one. The provision of supporting documentation throughout the development process is extremely vital, and should be considered as such.

* Software development tools which include such facilities as currently exist in the form of editors, compilers, etc. Tools are also going to be required in the areas of formal design methods, the underlying principle of which is that it can aid verification and validation through the use of automated techniques.

Example of such programming support environments can be found in UNIX's Programmer's Work Bench and the ADA Programming Support Environment, both of which are now briefly considered.

10.3.1 UNIX PROGRAMMER'S WORK BENCH

Although UNIX(trademark of Bell Labs) was originally intended for use by a few technically-oriented personnel it was soon realised that the system had the potential to cater for a much wider group of users. In particular it was realised that the text processing facilities of UNIX could be used in a number of ways other than program editing. This led to the development of the Programmer' Work Bench system (PWB) (Dolatta(1978)). In essence, PWB provides a working environment based upon a set of programming tools which are aimed at the development and administering of software destined for UNIX and non-UNIX based target systems.

The basic facilities incorporated within the PWB include remote job entry, the source code control system, text processing and document preparation tools. The remote job entry facilities provide the mechanism to support the transmission of software developed on the host to the target machine. It also supports the transferal of the results back to the user PWB for inspection. The source code control system provides a suite of commands that enables the users to control changes to a module's text. It records the incremental changes so that administrative control may be maintained over older release versions, test versions and current release versions.

The PWB system has, since inception, clearly demonstrated how such an environment can be effectively used in project management. Its development has been evolutionary - it was not designed and implemented as single cohesive facility. Each has been developed separately and incorporated into the existing set. Cohesiveness, and ensuring user friendliness, have been design issues which have safeguarded its success.

10.3.2 ADA PROGRAMMING SUPPORT ENVIRONMENT

Programming Support Environments (PSE), unlike the UNIX-PWB, have been based around a central database. In this way advantage is taken of the independence offered, from a sub-system interconnection viewpoint, and the experience gained from existing information retrieval systems. (The PWB is based on a specialised file-oriented approach which seriously restricts interconnection by a tool produced outside the development 'team')

PSE developments represent a different design philosophy whereby emphasis is being placed upon the design and construction of a complete environment. In this way careful consideration must be given at the outset to the individual tools to be provided, and their interaction with each other and the user.

The ADA language has been widely publicised (Ichbiah(1979) A) since 1979, as has its rationale (Ichbiah(1979) B). During the early days of the language design the U.S.A. Department Of Defense realised the importance of a programming support environment. After extensive discussion the proposals for an ADA Program Support Environment (APSE) were published in the STONEMAN document (USDOD(1980)).

The general requirements for an APSE include:

* the provision of tools which will support the ADA language from both technical and managerial viewpoints;

* tools to be provided for all stages of the software life cycle;

* individual tools to be constructed in such a manner that they can be easily connected to form part of an integrated environment;

* the environment to be easy to use with communication with the user

being based on a standard format.

Simplicity is the theme which appears throughout the APSE specification, and as such it only has three main consitituents:

* A database which acts as a central pool of information for each project.

* Interfaces for both the overall job control language and the database and individual tools.

* Tool-set which consists of all the tools that will be used throughout the software life cycle.

Portability is an important design issue for it not only maximises the user market for the language, but also provides for a flexible approach to its use between host machines, target machines and programmer teams. To reflect this important requirement the construction of the APSE is seen to be evolutionary with four incremental levels, as shown in figure 10.1. They are:

Level 0 - Host (or target) hardware and software.

Level 1 - Kernel ADA Program Support Environment (KAPSE) provides machine independent interfaces to level 0. It provides the framework upon which portability and environment re-hosting is based. As such it provides database, communication and run-time support functions.

Level 2 - Minimal ADA Program Support Environment (MAPSE) provides a minimal tool-set. They are considered necessary and sufficient for the development of ADA software. The tendency here is the provision of general purpose tools rather than specialised tools.

Level 3 - APSE will be constructed as an extension to the MAPSE to provide tools for the support of particular methodologies. In this way it is always seen to be open-ended so that it can evolve into different applications and ' never ' be obsolete.

A more detailed description of the APSE, and its history can be found in McDermid(1984), Buxton(1981), Stenning(1981).

10.3.3 INTEGRATED PROGRAMMING SUPPORT ENVIRONMENTS

There are at the present time two IPSE developments under way in the U.K: ECLIPSE and ASPECT (Alderson(1985), Hall(1985)). They both provide hardware and software combinations for the interconnection of a distributed PSE, and will incorporate formal methods.

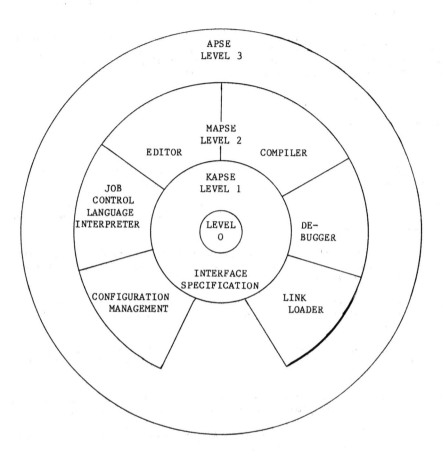

Fig. 10.1   APSE Structure

ASPECT provides a Public Tool Interface to encourage software tool developers to interconnect with their existing tool-set. Its design incorporates distribution of facilities between mainframes and individual workstations.

ECLIPSE has similar objectives which are centred around the use of an advanced database system specifically written to address the data management issues associated with software development. Both of these projects are in their early stages of development.

10.4 Summary

*   Formal methods have been introduced into the software development process to provide the foundation for analytical assessment.

*   Formal methods will be used throughout the development process by software designers, software writers, technical authors and test engineers alike.

*   There are basically two categories of formal method: model-oriented and property-oriented. They are characterised by the languages Z and Prolog respectively.

*   Because of the increase in softwarecomplexity, there will be a requirement for additional support tools which include those for formal methods.

*   Facilities will increase in sophistication to meet the demands made of them - this is reflected in the new title: Programming Support Environments.

*   Examples of two programming support environments are UNIX Programmer's Work Bench, and the ADA Programming Support Environment, APSE.

*   ASPECT and ECLIPSE are two Integrated Programming Support Environments (IPSE) currently under development in the U.K.

10.5 Things to Think About

*   Good programming used to be considered an art. How much 'creative pleasure' will be removed by the introduction of formal methods.

*   What other consequences will be associated with the move towards more scientific production of software?

*   Prioritise, from both the manager's and programmer's viewpoints, the features of a programming support environment.

* How could existing development tools provided on a microcomputer be enhanced to the level of the proposals for programming support environments? What difficulties might arise from the incompatibilities between different machine's capacities?

* What extensions might be made to the various layers in the APSE model of figure 10.1 to cope with distribution of software development over a wide geographical area?

Bibliography

"Something old, something new, something borrowed,
something blue"

Traditional: advice to a bride on what to wear

This bibliography contains both works referred to in the text, and some suggestions for further reading. The majority are quite new and should be easily obtainable; some are fairly old, and may have to be borrowed; none, to the authors' knowledge, are blue.

Abrial, J.R. (1982) "The Specification Language Z: Basic Library", Programming Research Group, Oxford, England, Internal Report.

Alderson, A. et al (1985), "An Overview of the ECLIPSE Project", in Integrated Project Support Environments, ed. J. McDermid, Peter Peregrinus pp. 100-113.

ALGOL (1982), "Revised Report on the Algorithmic Language ALGOL 60", J.W.Backus et al, Ed. Peter Naur,

Barnes, J. (1984), Programming in ADA, Addison Wesley.

Barron, D.W. (1986), "A Chip Off the Old Block - The Evolution of Software Engineering", Times Higher Education Supplement, 27/6/86.

Bowles, K.L. (1980), Beginner's Guide for the UCSD Pascal System, McGraw-Hill.

Brooks, F.P. Jr. (1975), The Mythical Man-month, Addison-Wesley.

Buxton,J.N. and Druffel, L.E. (1981) "Requirements for an ADA Programming Support Environment : Rationale for STONEMAN", in Software Engineering Environments, Ed. H. Hunke, North-Holland.

Cryer, N. and Cryer P. (1982), BASIC Programming on the BBC Microcomputer, Prentice-Hall.

DEFSTAN (1984), Guide to the Achievement of Quality in Software, 00-16/1, Ministry of Defence.

Dijkstra, E.W., Dahl, O.J. and Hoare, C.A.R. (1972), Structured Programming, Academic Press.

Dolatta, T.A. et al (1978), "The Programmer's Workbench", Bell Systems Technical Journal, Vol. 6 ,pp.2177-2200.

DTI (1985), The STARTS Guide: Software Tools for Application to large Real Time Systems, Department of Trade and Industry.

Dunn, R. and Ullmann, R. (1982), Quality Assurance for Computer Software, McGraw-Hill.

EEA (1983), Establishing a Quality Assurance Function for Software, Electronic Engineering Association.

EEA (1983), Software Configuration Management, Electronic Engineering Association.

Findlay, W. and Watt J. (1985), Pascal: An Introduction to Methodical Programming, 3rd edn., Pitman.

Gilb, T. (1976), Software Metrics, Chartwell-Bratt.

Goguen,J.A. et al (1977), "An Initial Algebra Approach to the Specification, Correctness and Implementation of Abstract Data Types", in Current Trends in Programming Methodology, Vol. IV - Data Structuring, Ed. R. T. Yeh, Prentice-Hall.

Hall, J.A. et al (1985), "An Overview of the ASPECT Architecture", in Integrated Project Support Environments, ed. J. McDermid, Peter Peregrinus, pp. 86-99.

Hayes, I. (1985), "Specifying the CICS Application Programmer's Interface", Technical Monograph PRG-47, Oxford University, England.

Higman, B. (1977), A Comparitive Study of Programming Languages, 2nd edn, Macdonald.

Ichbiah, J.D. et al (1979), "Preliminary ADA Reference Manual", ACM SIGPLAN Notices, Part A.

Ichbiah, J.D. et al (1979), "Rationale for the Design of the ADA Programming Language" ACM SIGPLAN Notices, Part B.

IEE(1985), Guidelines for the documentation of software in industrial computer systems, The Institution of Electrical Engineers.

Jackson, M. (1975), "Principles of Program Design", Academic Press.

Jackson, M.I. (1985), "Developing ADA Programs Using the Vienna Development Method", Software - Practice and Experience, Vol. 15, No. 3, pp. 305-318.

Jensen, K. and Wirth, N. (1975), Pascal User Manual and Report, 2nd edn, Springer-Verlag.

Kowalski, R. (1979), Logic for Problem Solving, North-Holland.

Morgan, C.C. and Sufrin, B.A. (1984), "Specification of the UNIX Filing System", IEEE Trans. Software Engineering, Vol. 10, No. 2, pp. 128-142.

McDermid, J. and Ripkin, K. (1984), Life Cycle Support in the ADA Environment, Cambridge University Press.

Myers, G. (1978), Composite Structured Design, Van Nostrand.

Myers, G. (1979), The Art of Software Testing, Wiley.

Parnas, D.L. (1972), "On the Criteria to be Used in Decomposing Systems into Modules", Comm. ACM, Vol. 15, No. 12, pp. 1053-1058.

Pratt, S.J. (1984), "Software Engineering and the Importance of Centralised Co-ordination in a Distributed Processing Environment", University Computing, Vol. 6, pp. 82-89.

Pratt, S.J. (1985), "Applicability of Decentralised/Centralised Control Procedures in Distributed Processing System Development and Operation", IEEE Trans. Engineering Management, Vol. EM-32, No. 3, pp. 116-123.

Pressman, R.S. (1982), Software Engineering : A Practitioner's Approach, McGraw-Hill.

Pugh, J.R. and Bell, D.H. (1983), Modern Methods for COBOL Programmers, Prentice-Hall.

Scientific American (1984), Computer Software, W.H. Freeman, New York.

Shooman, M.L. (1983), Software Engineering, McGraw-Hill.

Sommerville, I. (1985), Software Engineering 2nd Edn, Addison-Wesley.

Sorenson, I.H. (1982), "A Specification Language" in Program Specification, Vol. 134. Springer-Verlag, pp. 381-401.

Stenning, V. et al (1981), "The ADA Environment: A Perspective", COMPUTER, Vol. 14, No. 6, pp. 26-36.

Stuart, A. (1984), Writing and Analysing Effective Computer System Documentation, Holt, Rinehart and Winston.

US DOD (1980), "Reqirements for ADA Programming Support Environments, 'STONEMAN', U.S. Department of Defense.

Warnier, J.D. (1974), "Logical Construction of Programs", Van Nostrand.

Weinberg, G. (1971), The Psychology of Computer Programming, Van Nostrand.

Wirth, N. (1971), "Program Development by Stepwise Refinement", Comm. ACM, Vol.14 No.4, pp221-227.

Yourdon, E. and Constantine, L. (1979), Structured Design, Prentice-Hall.

Index